Culinary Creativity: Exploring Global Food Innovations

Josefina D. Drew

Published by Josefina D. Drew, 2024.

CULINARY CREATIVITY: EXPLORING GLOBAL FOOD INNOVATIONS

First edition. March 10, 2024.

Copyright © 2024 Josefina D. Drew.

ISBN: 979-8224715282

Written by Josefina D. Drew.

Table of Contents

The Evolution of Global Cuisine

Over the course of human history, the culinary landscape has continuously evolved, adapting to changing cultures, traditions, and technologies. Global cuisine, in particular, is representative of this evolution – a rich tapestry of flavors, techniques, and ingredients that have travelled across continents, oceans, and borders.

The story of global cuisine begins thousands of years ago when early humans began to cultivate crops and rear livestock. The emergence of agriculture marked a turning point in human history, allowing for the settling of communities and the development of food cultures. As these early civilizations flourished, food became more than just sustenance; it became a way to express creativity and identity.

Throughout ancient history, the exchange of goods and ideas between different cultures led to a mingling of culinary traditions. The Silk Road, for example, was a vast network of trade routes that connected the East and the West, facilitating the movement of spices, herbs, and other ingredients. This exchange not only influenced the development of culinary techniques but also laid the foundation for global cuisines we know today.

Fast forward to the Age of Exploration, a period marked by intrepid voyagers like Christopher Columbus, Vasco da Gama, and Ferdinand Magellan. These explorers set sail in search of new land, resources, and, of course, spices. Their discoveries opened up a whole new world of culinary possibilities as exotic ingredients such as cinnamon, cloves, and nutmeg made their way into European kitchens. This convergence of flavors from different continents sparked a culinary revolution, inspiring new dishes, techniques, and flavors.

In more recent history, the rapid advancement of transportation and communication has accelerated the evolution of global cuisine. The globalization era has made it easier than ever for people and cultures to connect, leading to an unprecedented exchange of culinary ideas.

Restaurateurs, celebrity chefs, and food bloggers have become ambassadors of global cuisine, showcasing the diversity and fusion of flavors through innovative creations.

Today, global cuisine has become an integral part of everyday life. Sushi, tacos, curry, and pasta - these dishes are now as commonplace as the local cuisine in many parts of the world. Migration and urbanization have contributed to the dissemination of different food cultures, bringing flavors from far-flung corners of the world to our local communities.

However, as global cuisine continues to evolve, it is important to recognize and celebrate its rich history and cultural significance. Each dish tells a story - a tale of the people, landscapes, and traditions that shaped it. The evolution of global cuisine reminds us of our shared humanity, our interconnectedness, and the incredible resilience of food cultures in the face of change.

In conclusion, the evolution of global cuisine is a testament to the human spirit - our endless curiosity, creativity, and adaptability. From the ancient trade routes of the Silk Road to the contemporary fusion cuisine of Michelin-starred restaurants, global cuisine embodies the intricate dance of cultures, ingredients, and flavors. It is a living, breathing testament to our collective gastronomic journey, telling a story that is as diverse and fascinating as the people who indulge in its creations.

The aim of this book is to provide readers with a comprehensive understanding of a particular subject or topic. It is intended to be informative, educational, and engaging, catering to both experts in the field and those who are new to the subject matter.

The scope of the book is wide, covering various aspects and subtopics related to the main subject. It may include historical context, current trends, theoretical frameworks, practical applications, and even future directions. The intention is to provide readers with a well-rounded understanding of the topic, leaving no stone unturned.

In order to achieve this aim, the book delves into detail on specific concepts, theories, models, and case studies. The author explores various perspectives, methodologies, and approaches relevant to the subject matter, encouraging critical thinking and analysis.

The book's level of detail may vary depending on its target audience and purpose. For academic texts, the writing may be highly detailed and include extensive citations to relevant literature and research. However, even non-academic books aim to provide detailed explanations and examples to enhance the reader's understanding and engagement.

The writing also aims to make complex information accessible to readers of diverse backgrounds and expertise. This may be achieved through clear explanations, simplified language where appropriate, and the use of relatable examples and analogies.

To keep readers engaged and interested, the book may incorporate interesting anecdotes, real-life examples, and thought-provoking questions. The author may also highlight controversies, debates, or areas of ongoing research related to the topic, stimulating further inquiry and discussion.

Overall, the goal of the book's aims and scope is to provide readers with a rich and comprehensive understanding of the subject at hand, fostering intellectual curiosity and promoting further exploration in the field.

Chapter 1: The Rise of Plant-Based Alternatives

In recent years, there has been a significant shift in consumer tastes and preferences towards plant-based alternatives. This growing trend is not just a passing fad but a movement that is here to stay. In this chapter, we will delve into the reasons behind this rising interest in plant-based foods and explore the historical context that has paved the way for their popularity.

1.1 The Environmental Impact of Animal Agriculture

One of the primary drivers of the plant-based movement is the growing awareness of the environmental impacts of animal agriculture. Livestock farming contributes significantly to greenhouse gas emissions, deforestation, and habitat destruction. As consumers become more conscious of their carbon footprint, they are increasingly turning to plant-based alternatives as a way to minimize their impact on the environment.

1.2 The Health Benefits of Plant-Based Diets

Another crucial aspect that has propelled the rise of plant-based alternatives is the increasing body of scientific research highlighting the health benefits of plant-based diets. Studies have shown that plant-based foods are rich in essential vitamins, minerals, and antioxidants that can promote overall well-being and reduce the risk of cardiovascular diseases and certain types of cancers. As a result, individuals are incorporating more plant-based options into their diets to improve their health and longevity.

1.3 Technological Advancements and the Rise of Meat Substitutes

In addition to the moral, ethical, and environmental concerns, the advancement of food technology has played a significant role in the popularity of plant-based alternatives. Innovations such as the Beyond Burger and the Impossible Burger have remarkably replicated the taste, texture, and aroma of traditional meat products. These technological breakthroughs have allowed consumers to satisfy their cravings for meat while enjoying a plant-based alternative.

1.4 Cultural and Societal Factors

The rise of plant-based alternatives can also be attributed to changing cultural and societal norms. Vegetarianism and veganism, once niche dietary choices, have now entered the mainstream and are being widely accepted and embraced. Celebrities, influencers, and social media platforms have played a vital role in normalized plant-based lifestyles and increasing their appeal to a broader audience.

1.5 The Diverse Array of Plant-Based Alternatives

Plant-based alternatives have come a long way from bland salads and platefuls of steamed vegetables. Today, there is an incredible variety of plant-based alternatives available, catering to every taste and culinary preference. From dairy-free milk and meat substitute options, to innovative plant-based desserts and snacks, consumers have never had such an extensive range of diverse, flavorful, and nutritious alternatives to choose from.

Conclusion

The rise of plant-based alternatives represents a seismic shift in the way we view and interact with food. Environmental concerns, health benefits, technological advancements, changing cultural norms, and a diverse array of options have all contributed to this growing trend. As the plant-based movement continues to gain momentum, it is shaping the way we eat and transforming the landscape of the food industry. In the following chapters, we will delve deeper into the various aspects of this movement and explore the impact it is having on individuals, businesses, and the planet as a whole.

1.1 History and Growth of Plant-Based Eating

Plant-based eating, also known as vegetarian or vegan diets, has been practiced for centuries by various cultures around the world. While many consider it a relatively modern phenomenon, plant-based diets have a long and fascinating history.

1.1.1 Ancient Roots

The roots of plant-based eating can be traced back to ancient civilizations such as the Greeks, Romans, and Indians. Philosophers and scholars in ancient Greece, such as Pythagoras, advocated for vegetarianism as a way to promote ethical reasoning and compassion for animals. Similarly, ancient Roman philosophers like Seneca and Plutarch also praised plant-based diets.

In India, the concept of plant-based eating has deep cultural and religious significance. Vegetarianism finds its roots in the ancient texts of Hinduism, where non-violence (ahimsa) is highly valued. Jainism, another Indian religion, takes non-violence to an even higher level by adhering to strict vegan principles.

1.1.2 Influence of Religions

Religious beliefs have played a significant role in shaping the growth of plant-based eating throughout history. Apart from Hinduism and Jainism, Buddhism also emphasizes kindness toward animals and promotes vegetarianism. The distribution of these religions to various parts of the world has contributed to the spread of vegetarianism and veganism.

Christianity, although historically more accepting of meat consumption, also has a vegetative tradition. Monastic orders in Europe, such as the Benedictines and Cistercians, often observed meatless days, and some monks and nuns adopted vegetarian diets as part of their religious practice.

1.1.3 Modern Plant-Based Movement

In more recent history, the plant-based movement gained momentum in the 19th and 20th centuries. The emergence of prominent advocates like Leo Tolstoy, Henry David Thoreau, and Mahatma Gandhi expanded discussions about ethical reasoning and the moral implications of consuming animal products.

The term vegetarian was coined in the mid-19th century by the British Vegetarian Society, which aimed to promote a meat-free lifestyle. The society's efforts led to the establishment of vegetarian restaurants, recipes, and books, further popularizing plant-based diets.

1.1.4 Health and Environmental Concerns

The growth of plant-based eating in the present day is fueled by a combination of health and environmental concerns. Research has emerged highlighting the potential health benefits of consuming primarily plant-based diets, including reduced risk of chronic diseases like heart disease and diabetes.

Additionally, concerns about animal welfare and the environmental impact of animal agriculture have gained significant attention. Increased awareness of factory farming practices and their detrimental effects on animal welfare and the environment has spurred people to adopt plant-based diets as a way to mitigate these issues.

1.1.5 The Rise of Veganism

Veganism, a stricter form of plant-based eating that excludes all animal products, has also experienced rapid growth in recent years. The shift toward veganism is not only related to health and ethical concerns but also to advancements in plant-based food alternatives. The development of meat and dairy substitutes, such as fortified plant-based milks and burgers, has made it easier for individuals to adopt veganism without sacrificing their favorite foods.

In conclusion, plant-based eating has a rich and varied history that dates back to ancient civilizations and is influenced by cultural, religious, health, and environmental factors. From the ethical reasoning of ancient Greek philosophers to the flourishing vegan movement of today, plant-based diets continue to evolve and gain popularity as more individuals recognize the benefits they offer to both personal well-being and the planet.

1. Creator of the Impossible Burger

One of the key innovations in plant-based meat is the creation of the Impossible Burger. This burger was developed by the company Impossible Foods, which sought to create a vegetarian burger that would replicate the taste and texture of meat. The key innovation behind this burger lies in the inclusion of a protein called heme, which gives meat its distinctive taste. By isolating heme from plants and including it in their burger, Impossible Foods was able to create a plant-based alternative that closely mimics beef.

2. Advancements in Texturing Techniques

Another important innovation in the realm of plant-based meats is the advancement in texturing techniques. Historically, plant-based proteins have struggled to replicate the fibrous texture found in traditional meat products. However, in recent years, companies have made significant progress in creating plant-based meats with a realistic texture. They accomplish this by using various techniques such as extrusion, grinding, and molding to create structures that closely resemble animal muscle fibers. These advancements have contributed to the increasing acceptance and popularity of plant-based meat products.

3. Fermentation for Dairy Alternatives

Plant-based dairy alternatives have also seen key innovations, particularly in the area of fermentation. One standout example is the use of microbial fermentation to produce non-dairy milk alternatives such as plant-based yogurt, kefir, and cheese. Many dairy alternatives on the market today are made by fermenting plant proteins, like peas, oats, or soy, with bacterial cultures.

This process creates flavors and textures that resemble the taste and consistency of traditional dairy products. Through fermentation, companies are able to enhance the nutritional profile while also providing a satisfying alternative for those seeking to avoid animal-based products.

4. Cultured Meat: The Future of Plant-Based Protein?

One of the most anticipated innovations in plant-based meat is the development of cultured meat. This involves creating meat products from animal cells grown in a lab, without the need for traditional animal agriculture. While cultured meat is not entirely plant-based, it represents a groundbreaking approach to produce meat using significantly fewer resources and without harming animals. Although it is still in the early stages of development, with prototypes being introduced to the market, its potential to revolutionize the food industry and reduce environmental impact cannot be overlooked.

In summary, key innovations in plant-based meat and dairy include the creation of the Impossible Burger, advancements in texturing techniques for realistic meat substitutes, the use of fermentation in plant-based dairy alternatives, and the promising future of cultured meat. These developments have played a crucial role in expanding the options available to consumers seeking sustainable and cruelty-free alternatives to conventional animal products.

Health and Environmental Impacts of different factors can have both immediate and long-term effects on individuals and the environment as a whole. It is important to recognize and understand these impacts so that proactive measures can be implemented to prevent or minimize harm. In this article, we will delve into the various factors contributing to health and environmental impacts and explore the consequences they entail.

One of the most prominent factors that affect both human health and the environment is pollution. Pollution comes in many forms, including air pollution, water pollution, and soil pollution. Each type has its unique set of health and environmental consequences. Air pollution, for instance, can lead to respiratory issues, such as asthma and chronic obstructive pulmonary disease (COPD). Additionally, prolonged exposure to polluted air has been linked to heart disease, stroke, and even certain types of cancer. From an environmental standpoint, air pollution contributes to the depletion of the ozone layer and contributes to global warming.

Water pollution has equally devastating effects on both human health and the environment. Consuming contaminated water can result in various waterborne diseases, including cholera, dysentery, and hepatitis A. Additionally, contaminated water can harm aquatic ecosystems, leading to the death of marine life and disrupting the natural balance. Furthermore, water pollution can seep into the ground, contaminating underground water sources and making them unfit for consumption or agricultural use.

Another factor contributing to health and environmental impacts is deforestation. Cutting down trees on a large scale disrupts delicate ecosystems and leads to a loss of biodiversity. Forests play a vital role in regulating air quality by absorbing carbon dioxide and releasing oxygen. With deforestation, there is an alarming increase in greenhouse gases, exacerbating the effects of climate change. Furthermore, deforestation impacts local communities that rely on forests for their livelihoods, affecting their socio-economic well-being.

Agricultural practices, particularly those associated with intensive farming, also have significant health and environmental impacts. The use of chemical fertilizers, pesticides, and herbicides contaminates soil, water, and air. Prolonged exposure to these chemicals can lead to chronic health conditions and even cancer in humans. Moreover, agricultural runoff containing these toxic substances flows into nearby water bodies, resulting in the degradation of water quality and the loss of aquatic life.

Climate change is another crucial factor that impacts both health and the environment. Rising global temperatures, extreme weather events, and sea-level rise are all consequences of climate change. These changes have severe implications for human health, including increased heat-related illnesses, the spread of infectious diseases, and food and water insecurity. From an environmental perspective, climate change disrupts natural habitats, exacerbates deforestation, and threatens species survival.

The identification of these health and environmental impacts is just the first step towards addressing them. It is vital for governments, organizations, and individuals to take action in reducing pollution levels, promoting sustainable practices, implementing climate change mitigation strategies, and educating communities about the importance of their roles in safeguarding the environment and overall well-being. By doing so, we can create a healthier and more sustainable future for generations to come.

Case studies are an effective way to understand the strategies and success stories of brands that have adopted a plant-based approach. These brands have not only managed to meet the demands of a growing consumer base but have also made significant contributions to promoting sustainability and a healthier lifestyle. In this section, we will explore some notable case studies of successful plant-based brands and delve into their growth stories.

1. Beyond Meat: Beyond Meat is a trailblazer in the plant-based industry. This brand has gained immense popularity for its meat substitute products, which not only replicate the taste and texture of actual meat but also have a smaller environmental impact. Beyond Meat has managed to secure partnerships with major foodservice chains like Subway, Pizza Hut, and McDonald's, allowing them to reach a larger audience. Their strategic approach to marketing, which involved partnerships with high-profile athletes and celebrities, has further contributed to their success. With a consistently expanding product range and a focus on innovation, Beyond Meat has become a go-to brand for those looking to adopt a plant-based diet.

2. Impossible Foods: Another major player in the plant-based market is Impossible Foods. The brand is particularly famous for its Impossible Burger, a plant-based patty designed to mimic the taste, texture, and experience of traditional beef burgers. Impossible Foods has leveraged technological advancements to create a product that appeals to both vegetarians and meat-eaters. The brand has actively collaborated with restaurants and fast-food chains to incorporate their products into their menus. Their partnership with Burger King, which launched the Impossible Whopper, is a testament to their market penetration. By focusing on taste, texture, and sustainability, Impossible Foods has successfully established itself as a leading plant-based brand.

3. Oatly: Oatly has managed to carve a unique space for itself in the plant-based movement by offering dairy alternatives made from oats. Their oat milk products have gained popularity due to their creamy texture and neutral taste, making them a versatile choice for various beverages and recipes. Oatly was successful in strategizing their marketing campaign, engaging with consumers through social media platforms and word-of-mouth. Oatly's commitment to sustainable practices, such as sourcing oats from environmentally responsible farms, has resonated with ecologically conscious consumers. The demand for their products led to considerable growth, pushing

Oatly to expand their distribution to supermarkets and coffee shops worldwide. The brand's unique positioning, memorable branding, and focus on sustainability have propelled it to success in the plant-based market.

4. Silk: Silk, a leading plant-based dairy alternative brand, offers a wide range of products, including almond milk, soy milk, and coconut milk. Silk has capitalized on several trends within the plant-based movement, positioning their products as healthier alternatives to traditional dairy. Their marketing campaigns highlighting the environmental benefits of plant-based milk and the health advantages of its alternatives have strongly resonated with consumers. Silk's ability to adapt to changing consumer demands by continually introducing new products and embracing trends like protein fortification has allowed them to maintain a competitive edge in the market. The brand's commitment to providing high-quality, delicious products has resulted in widespread distribution across supermarkets and stores globally.

In conclusion, these case studies demonstrate the success of plant-based brands that have managed to disrupt traditional markets with innovative and sustainable products. Whether it is by simulating the taste and texture of animal-based products or by providing healthier and environmentally friendly alternatives, these brands have effectively captured consumer attention and driven substantial growth. Their strategic brand positioning, marketing campaigns, product diversification, and focus on sustainability have made them leaders in the plant-based movement. These case studies serve as inspiration for aspiring plant-based brands and offer valuable insights into the strategies behind their success.

Chapter 2: Fermentation – A Resurgence

In recent years, there has been a remarkable resurgence in the age-old practice of fermentation. From sourdough bread and craft beer to kimchi and kombucha, fermented foods and beverages have gained immense popularity and become staples in numerous cuisines worldwide. This resurgence may seem like a modern trend, but fermentation is a historical and cross-cultural tradition that spans thousands of years.

The process of fermentation involves the conversion of sugars and carbohydrates into alcohol or organic acids, carried out by microscopic organisms called microorganisms. These include bacteria, yeasts, and molds, which break down the complex molecules in foods and produce byproducts that give fermented products their unique flavors, textures, and health benefits.

Fermentation offers a natural way to preserve foods, making them resistant to spoilage by harmful bacteria and increasing their shelf life. Before the advent of refrigeration and modern preservation techniques, fermentation played a vital role in sustaining communities throughout the year, particularly during winter months when fresh produce was scarce.

Today, the resurgence of fermentation can be attributed to a multitude of factors. Firstly, there is a growing interest in the quality and authenticity of foods. Consumers are becoming increasingly conscious of the ingredients used in their food and are seeking out natural, simple, and time-honored methods of preparation. Fermentation fits into this narrative perfectly, as it allows for minimal processing and the preservation of natural flavors and nutrients.

Another driving force behind the fermentation resurgence is the growing body of scientific research supporting the health benefits of fermented foods. These natural probiotics help support a healthy gut microbiome, which in turn aids digestion and strengthens the immune system. As more people become aware of the link between gut health and overall well-being, the demand for fermented foods continues to rise.

Furthermore, fermentation aligns with the current sustainability movement. As people seek to reduce waste and make the most of their resources, fermentation offers a way to utilize surplus or less desirable ingredients. Ugly vegetables, overripe fruit, and leftover grains can all find a new life through fermentation, reducing food waste and promoting a more sustainable food system.

With the revival of ancient techniques and flavors, fermentation has also become a part of the movement towards a more local and connected food culture. Artisanal fermenters have sprung up all over the world, honoring traditional methods while experimenting with new ingredients and flavors. This grassroots fermentation movement builds community, fosters culinary creativity, and celebrates diversity in taste and tradition.

Finally, the rise of social media has undoubtedly played a significant role in boosting the popularity of fermented foods. Aesthetically pleasing photos and tantalizing recipes shared on platforms like Instagram and Pinterest have sparked curiosity and inspired individuals to try their hand at fermentation. The online fermentation community has created a space for enthusiasts to share their experiences, troubleshoot issues, and continue learning and experimenting with this ancient practice.

In conclusion, fermentation has made a triumphant comeback in recent years. Its ability to preserve food naturally, promote health, align with sustainability values, revitalize ancient food traditions, and connect communities has captured the interest and passion of people worldwide. As we continue to appreciate the craftsmanship and complexity of fermented foods and beverages, it is clear that fermentation is no fleeting trend but a timeless culinary art with a powerful cultural and scientific foundation.

Traditional fermentation techniques have been practiced by various cultures around the world for centuries. These techniques involve the transformation of raw ingredients into flavorful and preserved foods and beverages through the action of beneficial microorganisms.

One of the most well-known traditional fermentation techniques is used to produce dairy products such as yogurt and cheese. In yogurt production, milk is heated and then inoculated with a starter culture containing lactic acid bacteria. These bacteria ferment the lactose in the milk into lactic acid, which gives yogurt its characteristic tangy flavor and thick texture. Similarly, in cheese production, specific strains of bacteria and mold are added to milk to encourage fermentation, resulting in the formation of curds.

In eastern Asian countries like Japan and Korea, traditional fermentation techniques are used to produce staples such as soy sauce, miso, and kimchi. Soy sauce is made by fermenting soybeans and wheat with the help of the fungus Aspergillus and a specific strain of yeast. The fermentation process breaks down the proteins and carbohydrates in the soybeans, resulting in a savory and flavorful sauce. Miso, on the other hand, is produced by fermenting soybeans with salt and a specific mold, resulting in a paste-like condiment with a distinctive umami flavor.

Kimchi, a popular Korean fermented side dish, is made by lacto-fermentation of vegetables such as napa cabbage, radishes, and scallions. It involves a two-step process: salting the vegetables to draw out moisture and then fermenting them in a spicy brine mixture. Lactic acid bacteria are responsible for the fermentation process, giving kimchi its unique tanginess and complex flavors.

In many African countries, traditional fermentation techniques are practiced to preserve and enhance the flavors of grains, seeds, and tubers. For example, in Ethiopia, teff, a gluten-free grain, is used to make the traditional fermented bread called injera. Teff flour is mixed with water and left to ferment for several days, resulting in a slightly tangy and spongy bread that is an essential part of the Ethiopian diet.

Similarly, in West Africa, a popular fermented product is made from cassava, a starchy tuber. The cassava roots are peeled, grated, and soaked in water for a few days until fermentation occurs. This process enhances the flavors and reduces the toxins present in raw cassava, making it safe to be consumed.

These examples illustrate the vast variety of traditional fermentation techniques practiced globally. They not only serve as methods of preservation but also impart unique flavors and textures to the final products. These techniques have been passed down through generations, preserving cultural traditions and providing individuals with a connection to their ancestral heritage. Today, many of these traditional fermented foods continue to be valued for their taste, nutritional benefits, and contribution to gastronomy.

2.2 Modern Fermentation and Health

Fermentation is an ancient food preservation and preparation technique that has been utilized by humans for thousands of years. While traditional fermentation methods involve the use of bacteria and yeasts, modern fermentation practices have evolved to incorporate scientific advancements and technological innovations. In recent years, fermentation has gained significant attention due to its potential health benefits, which have sparked the interest and curiosity of researchers, food enthusiasts, and consumers alike.

One of the key factors in the popularity of fermentation is its association with gut health. The human gut is home to a diverse community of microorganisms, collectively known as the gut microbiota. These microorganisms play a crucial role in maintaining our overall health, as they are involved in the digestion and absorption of nutrients, production of vitamins, modulation of the immune system, and even the regulation of mood and mental health. The consumption of fermented foods has been linked to an improvement in gut microbiota diversity and composition, which can have numerous positive effects on our well-being.

Yogurt is perhaps one of the most well-known fermented foods that is widely recognized for its health benefits. Yogurt is made through a process in which milk is fermented by the action of lactic acid bacteria, such as Lactobacillus and Streptococcus thermophilus. These bacteria convert lactose, the primary sugar in milk, into lactic acid. This process not only gives yogurt its distinct tangy taste, but also creates an environment that is favorable for the growth and survival of beneficial probiotic bacteria, which confer various health benefits upon consumption.

Probiotics, the beneficial live bacteria found in fermented foods like yogurt, have been shown to have numerous positive effects on gut health. They have been found to aid in digestion, enhance nutrient absorption, strengthen the gut barrier, and inhibit the growth of harmful bacteria. Regular consumption of yogurt and other probiotic-rich foods has also been associated with a reduced risk of various gastrointestinal disorders, including diarrhea, irritable bowel syndrome, and inflammatory bowel disease. Additionally, studies have revealed potential links between probiotic consumption and improved mental health, as certain strains of bacteria have been found to influence the production of neurotransmitters in the gut, which can affect mood and emotions.

Apart from yogurt, other fermented foods that have gained popularity in recent years include sauerkraut, kimchi, miso, and kombucha. These foods are produced through the natural process of lacto-fermentation, whereby beneficial bacteria convert the innate sugars and starches present in the raw ingredients into lactic acid. This process not only leads to the characteristic sour taste of these foods, but also increases their nutritional value. Fermented vegetables, such as sauerkraut and kimchi, serve as excellent sources of vitamin C and fiber. Miso, a fermented soybean paste commonly used in Japanese cuisine, is rich in essential amino acids and vitamins. Kombucha, a fizzy fermented tea, contains various organic acids, antioxidants, and beneficial enzymes that contribute to its potential health benefits.

It is important to note that not all fermented foods possess the same health benefits. While the majority of fermented foods are safe to consume and can provide a range of positive effects on gut health, the presence of added sugars, preservatives, or the use of unhygienic fermentation practices can diminish their nutritional value and even pose certain health risks. Therefore, it is advisable to choose fermented foods that are made using natural ingredients and traditional fermentation methods to reap the maximum health advantages.

In conclusion, modern fermentation practices have brought ancient food preservation techniques to new heights. The health benefits associated with the consumption of fermented foods, particularly those rich in probiotics, have sparked widespread interest and attention. From improving gut health and digestion to enhancing overall well-being and mental health, the scientific research supports the positive impact of fermented foods on human health. As more studies are conducted and technology advances, we can expect to further unlock the potential health benefits of fermentation and continue to incorporate them into our modern diets.

Fermented foods have been part of culinary traditions for centuries, with people from different cultures recognizing their unique flavors and health benefits. However, in recent years, there has been a surge of interest in fermented foods in the culinary world. Chefs and food enthusiasts are exploring the creative potential of fermentation, leading to innovative dishes and new taste experiences.

One of the reasons for this renewed interest in fermented foods is the growing understanding of their health benefits. Fermentation is a natural process in which microorganisms, such as bacteria, yeasts, and molds, break down the carbohydrates in food, converting them into acids, alcohol, or gases. This process not only enhances the flavor and texture of the food but also increases its nutritional value. The microorganisms involved in fermentation produce enzymes and probiotic bacteria, which aid digestion and support a healthy gut microbiome.

Chefs are taking this knowledge and using fermentation techniques to elevate their dishes. For example, traditional fermented foods like kimchi, sauerkraut, and miso are being used in innovative ways to add complex flavors and unique dimensions to meals. Instead of just being sides or condiments, fermented foods are becoming central elements in dishes. Fermented vegetables can be used as toppings for pizza or added to pasta sauces for a tangy and rich twist. Fermented soybeans can be used to create umami-rich glazes or marinades for meats and vegetables.

Apart from traditional fermented foods, chefs are also experimenting with lesser-known items like kefir, tempeh, and kombucha. These probiotic-rich foods are being used as bases for sauces, dressings, and marinades, providing a unique depth of flavor and introducing interesting textures. For example, tempeh, a fermented soybean cake, is being sliced and used as a meat substitute in sandwiches, while kombucha, a fermented tea, is being used as a base for creative cocktails and mocktails.

Furthermore, fermentation is not limited to fruits and vegetables. Chefs are pushing the boundaries by fermenting various ingredients like grains, nuts, and dairy products. For instance, yogurt is being transformed into tangy cream sauces, and fermented oats are being used to create creamy and savory risotto-style dishes. Fermented nuts and seeds are being ground into flavorful spreads and pastes that can be used in desserts or as a base for dressings.

Fermentation techniques are not restricted to savory foods either. Pastry chefs are experimenting with fermented doughs and batters for bread, cakes, and pastries. Fermented doughs provide a distinctive and yeasty flavor, as well as improved texture and tenderness. Furthermore, the microorganisms present in fermented doughs can enhance shelf life and make baked goods more digestible.

In conclusion, fermented foods are gaining popularity in culinary innovation due to their unique flavor profiles and numerous health benefits.

Chefs are exploring their potential, using them as main ingredients and incorporating them into various dishes. From adding depth to traditional recipes to creating entirely new taste experiences, fermentation is driving culinary innovation in exciting and delicious ways.

Commercial fermentation refers to the large-scale production of microorganisms or their metabolites for various commercial purposes. This process has gained significant popularity in recent years due to the increasing demand for fermented products such as food and beverages, industrial enzymes, pharmaceuticals, and agricultural products. However, despite its promising potential, commercial fermentation also poses several challenges that need to be addressed. In this article, we will explore these challenges as well as the opportunities they present in the field of commercial fermentation.

One of the major challenges faced in commercial fermentation is the selection and optimization of the fermenting microorganism. Different microorganisms have different metabolic capabilities and growth requirements. Therefore, finding the most suitable microorganism for a specific fermentation process requires careful consideration of factors such as the desired product, the fermentation conditions, and the available resources. Additionally, optimizing the growth conditions, such as temperature, pH, and nutrient availability, is crucial to maximize productivity and efficiency.

Another significant challenge in commercial fermentation is the contamination risk. Fermentation processes often provide favorable conditions for the growth of unwanted microorganisms, which can result in product spoilage or reduced productivity. Preventing contamination requires strict hygienic practices, as well as the use of advanced sterilization techniques. Moreover, monitoring the fermentation process in real-time using sensor technologies can enable early detection of contamination events and prompt action.

Additionally, scalability is a critical issue in commercial fermentation. Up-scaling a fermentation process from lab-scale to industrial-scale poses numerous challenges due to the differences in equipment, mixing, and mass transfer capabilities. Insufficient scaling-up can result in variations in the fermentation performance and ultimately affect the quality and consistency of the final product. Overcoming scalability issues requires careful planning, process optimization, and the implementation of appropriate engineering solutions.

Furthermore, ensuring product quality and consistency throughout large-scale fermentation processes is essential for commercial success. Changes in fermentation conditions or microorganism performance can lead to variations in product composition and quality. Implementing robust quality control protocols, such as regular sampling and testing, is essential to detect any variations and ensure product consistency. Utilizing process analytical technologies (PAT), such as spectroscopy and chromatography, can provide real-time feedback on critical quality attributes and enable process adjustments as needed.

Despite these challenges, commercial fermentation also presents several exciting opportunities. The growing trend towards natural and sustainable ingredients in various industries has fueled the demand for fermentation-based products. Microbial fermentation offers a more environmentally friendly and cost-effective alternative to traditional chemical synthesis processes, reducing the reliance on non-renewable resources. Moreover, advancements in genetic engineering and synthetic biology have opened up new possibilities for tailored fermentation processes, enabling the production of novel and specialized products.

The use of non-conventional microorganisms in commercial fermentation is also gaining attention. Beyond the traditional use of bacteria and yeasts, new types of microorganisms such as filamentous fungi and extremophiles offer unique metabolic capabilities and the potential to produce valuable compounds. Exploring and harnessing the untapped potential of these microorganisms can lead to the development of innovative and desirable products with diverse applications.

In conclusion, commercial fermentation presents significant challenges and opportunities. Addressing the challenges of microorganism selection, contamination prevention, scalability, and product quality control is crucial for successful commercial fermentation processes. On the other hand, exploring the potential of sustainable practices, genetic engineering, and non-conventional microorganisms can open up new avenues for innovative and high-value fermentation products. Overcoming these challenges and capitalizing on the opportunities will pave the way for the continued growth and advancement of commercial fermentation in various industries.

Chapter 3: Functional Foods and Superfoods

In recent years, there has been a growing interest in functional foods and superfoods. These terms have become buzzwords in the field of nutrition, often associated with various health benefits. But what exactly are functional foods and superfoods? And what sets them apart from regular foods? In this chapter, we will delve into the world of functional foods and superfoods, exploring their unique qualities and the science behind their potential health benefits.

Defining Functional Foods:

Functional foods are defined as foods that provide health benefits beyond basic nutrition. They are designed to improve one's health status, reduce the risk of chronic diseases, or enhance overall well-being. Unlike regular foods, which are consumed primarily for their basic nutritional content, functional foods may contain additional bioactive components, such as probiotics, prebiotics, antioxidants, or phytochemicals.

Functional foods can be either naturally occurring or fortified with added nutrients or biologically active substances. For example, yogurt enriched with probiotics is considered a functional food, as it provides beneficial bacteria that can improve gut health. Other examples include foods fortified with omega-3 fatty acids for heart health or plant sterols for cholesterol reduction.

Superfoods Explained:

Superfoods are a subset of functional foods that are particularly nutrient-dense and packed with beneficial compounds. They are often touted for their high levels of vitamins, minerals, and antioxidants. Superfoods can be derived from both plant and animal sources, and examples include berries, leafy greens, fatty fish, nuts, seeds, and whole grains.

These foods are often celebrated for their potential to fight inflammation, boost the immune system, improve brain health, and provide an array of other health benefits. However, it's important to note that the term superfood is not a scientific term, and its usage can sometimes be ambiguous or misleading. While some superfoods have proven health benefits, others may be glorified without sufficient scientific evidence to support their claims.

The Science Behind Superfoods:

Many superfoods owe their touted health benefits to the rich levels of antioxidants they contain. Antioxidants are compounds that neutralize harmful free radicals in the body, reducing oxidative stress and inflammation. For instance, berries like blueberries and cranberries are loaded with antioxidants known as anthocyanins, which have been linked to numerous health benefits, including improved brain function and reduced risk of heart disease.

Certain superfoods also boast high levels of essential nutrients, such as omega-3 fatty acids found in fatty fish like salmon, which are known for their anti-inflammatory properties. Additionally, superfoods like kale and spinach are excellent sources of vitamins and minerals that support overall health and provide numerous physiological benefits.

FUNCTIONAL FOODS AND superfoods play a distinct role in a healthy diet. By consuming these foods, individuals can go beyond fulfilling their basic nutritional requirements and potentially gain additional health benefits. However, it's essential to approach the subject with caution and rely on scientific evidence rather than marketing hype. While many superfoods have proven health benefits, it's important to consume a varied diet that includes a wide array of nutrients to achieve overall good health.

In recent years, there has been much talk about functional foods and superfoods. These terms are often used interchangeably, but they have different meanings and implications. In order to better understand these concepts, it is important to define what they actually refer to.

Functional foods are defined as natural or processed foods that contain unique compounds which provide specific health benefits beyond the basic nutritional value. These foods are often enriched or fortified with additional nutrients or bioactive substances that promote various physiological functions in the body. Functional foods can come in different forms, including whole foods, fortified foods, and dietary supplements.

Superfoods, on the other hand, are a subset of functional foods that are particularly rich in nutrients and antioxidants, making them beneficial for health. Although there is no formal definition or specific scientific criteria for superfoods, these foods are commonly recognized for their exceptional nutrient density and health-promoting properties. They are typically high in vitamins, minerals, phytochemicals, or other bioactive compounds that are believed to provide numerous health benefits.

Some popular examples of functional foods include probiotic yogurt, whole grains fortified with vitamins and minerals, and soy-based foods enriched with isoflavones. These foods provide additional health benefits beyond their basic nutritional components. Probiotic yogurt, for instance, contains beneficial bacteria that support a healthy digestive system and boost the immune system. Fortified whole grains provide essential vitamins and minerals that may be lacking in a typical diet. Soy-based foods fortified with isoflavones may contribute to lowering the risk of certain chronic diseases, such as cardiovascular disease and certain types of cancers.

Now let's turn our attention to superfoods. Blueberries, often regarded as one of the ultimate superfoods, are packed with antioxidants and phytochemicals that support brain health and exhibit anti-inflammatory properties. Spinach, another commonly recognized superfood, is rich in vitamins A, C, K, iron, and other essential nutrients that promote bone health, strengthen immune function, and protect against chronic diseases. Salmon is often considered a superfood due to its high content of omega-3 fatty acids, which are essential for heart health, brain function, and reducing the risk of chronic inflammation.

It is important to note that although functional foods and superfoods may offer various health benefits, they should not be considered as a magic solution for optimal health. A well-balanced diet that includes a variety of foods is crucial for overall well-being. Incorporating functional foods and superfoods into a healthy diet, however, can be a great way to enhance nutrition and potentially reduce the risk of certain diseases.

In conclusion, functional foods are natural or processed foods that contain unique compounds providing specific health benefits beyond basic nutrition, while superfoods are a subset of functional foods known for their exceptional nutrient density and health-promoting properties. By understanding the definition and distinguishing between these two terms, individuals can make informed choices about incorporating these types of foods into their diet for overall health benefits.

Global superfoods are nutrient-rich foods that are considered to be highly beneficial for health and well-being. They have gained popularity in recent years as people become more conscious of the importance of including nutritious foods in their diet. These superfoods come from various cultural origins and have their own unique set of nutrients and health benefits.

One such example of a global superfood is quinoa, which originated in the Andean regions of South America. Quinoa is a tiny grain-like seed that is rich in protein, fiber, and various vitamins and minerals. It is gluten-free and has a low glycemic index, making it suitable for those with gluten sensitivity or diabetes. Quinoa is widely regarded as a complete protein, meaning it contains all nine essential amino acids required by the body. It is also a good source of antioxidants, which can help protect against oxidative stress and inflammation.

Another global superfood with cultural origins from Japan is matcha green tea. Matcha is made from ground-up green tea leaves and is known for its vibrant green color. It is packed with antioxidants called catechins, which have been linked to a reduced risk of chronic diseases such as heart disease and certain types of cancer. Matcha also contains a compound called L-theanine, which promotes relaxation and mental clarity. This is why matcha is often used in meditation practices like tea ceremonies.

Moving on to the Middle East, we find another global superfood called pomegranate. Pomegranates have a rich cultural significance in this region and have been consumed for centuries. The delicious seeds are packed with fiber, vitamins C and K, and antioxidants. The antioxidants in pomegranates, particularly punicalagins, have been shown to have potent anti-inflammatory and anti-aging properties. Research suggests that consuming pomegranate or its juice may help reduce blood pressure, lower LDL cholesterol, and improve overall heart health.

Lastly, we cannot talk about global superfoods without mentioning the acai berry from Brazil. This small purple fruit has gained worldwide attention for its exceptional antioxidant profile. It is particularly rich in anthocyanins, which give it its intense color and provide a wide range of health benefits. Acai berries have been linked to improved brain function, reduced inflammation, and enhanced immune function. They are often consumed in smoothies, bowls, or as a powdered supplement.

In conclusion, global superfoods come from diverse cultural origins and offer a wide array of nutrients and health benefits. Quinoa from South America, matcha green tea from Japan, pomegranates from the Middle East, and acai berries from Brazil are just a few examples of these powerful foods. Incorporating these superfoods into our diets can be a delicious and effective way to support long-term health and well-being.

Scientific research has provided numerous insights into the health benefits of various practices. These insights have not only helped improve our understanding of the human body but have also guided the development of new treatments and interventions. In this section, we will explore some of the key findings in the field of health benefits.

One of the most studied areas is the impact of physical activity on health. Regular exercise has been shown to have a multitude of benefits, including reducing the risk of chronic diseases such as cardiovascular disease, diabetes, and certain types of cancer. Exercise also helps maintain a healthy body weight, strengthens muscles and bones, improves mood, and enhances cognitive function. Furthermore, recent research has demonstrated that physical activity can even affect gene expression, leading to favorable changes in our genetic makeup.

In addition to physical activity, nutrition plays a crucial role in maintaining optimal health. Scientific studies have demonstrated the importance of a balanced diet, rich in fruits, vegetables, whole grains, lean proteins, and healthy fats. Such a diet provides essential nutrients, vitamins, and minerals that support various bodily functions. Conversely, a diet high in processed foods, added sugars, and unhealthy fats has been linked to increased risk of obesity, heart disease, diabetes, and other chronic conditions.

Recent scientific research has also shed light on the significance of sleep in promoting health and well-being. Sleep plays a vital role in cognitive function, memory consolidation, and the immune system's functionality. Insufficient sleep has been associated with an increased risk of chronic conditions such as obesity, diabetes, cardiovascular disease, and mental health disorders. In contrast, adequate and restful sleep has been shown to improve mood, enhance cognitive performance, and bolster the immune system.

Furthermore, studies have investigated the benefits of mindfulness and meditation on mental and physical health. Mindfulness practices have been found to reduce stress, anxiety, and depression. They also improve emotional well-being, attention, and self-awareness. Moreover, mindfulness-based interventions have shown promise in managing pain, reducing blood pressure, boosting the immune system, and even modulating gene expression.

Advancements in technology have paved the way for new insights into the relationship between the mind and body. The emerging field of psychoneuroimmunology explores how psychological factors, such as stress and emotions, impact the immune system and overall health. The mind-body connection is now recognized as an integral aspect of health and plays a role in conditions such as chronic pain, gastrointestinal disorders, and autoimmune diseases.

It is evident that scientific research has provided substantial evidence on the numerous benefits of various practices. This knowledge empowers individuals to make informed lifestyle choices that promote their overall health and well-being. As scientists continue to investigate and uncover more insights, we can expect further advancements in the field of understanding health benefits and how to harness them to improve our lives.

Market Trends:

The market trends in today's industry play a crucial role in shaping consumer behavior and making informed business decisions. Understanding and analyzing these trends can help businesses stay competitive and adapt to ever-changing consumer demands. Here are some of the current market trends that are influencing consumer behavior:

1. Digital Transformation: The rapid advancement of technology is bringing about a digital revolution in almost all industries. As consumers integrate technology into their everyday lives, businesses need to embrace digital transformation to engage with customers effectively. This includes mobile apps, online shopping, personalized marketing strategies, and the use of AI-powered chatbots for customer service. Consumer behavior is increasingly leaning towards digital platforms, creating opportunities for businesses to connect with their target audience online.

2. Sustainability and Social Responsibility: Today's consumers are becoming increasingly conscious of the environmental and social impact of

their purchasing decisions. They are more likely to support businesses that demonstrate sustainable practices and social responsibility. This trend has led to the rise of eco-friendly products, vegan alternatives, and companies implementing ethical sourcing and production methods. Understanding and promoting sustainable practices can attract a growing segment of environmentally-conscious consumers.

3. Personalization: With the abundance of information available, consumers now expect personalized experiences. Businesses that can effectively tailor their products, services, and customer interactions based on individual preferences are more likely to succeed. AI and data analytics have made it easier for companies to gather consumer data and deliver personalized marketing messages, recommendations, and offers. Consumer behavior has responded positively to personalized approaches, with increased engagement and loyalty from customers.

Consumer Behavior:

Consumer behavior refers to the decision-making process and actions taken by individuals when purchasing goods or services. Understanding consumer behavior is vital for businesses as it helps them tailor their marketing strategies, improve customer experiences, and develop long-term relationships with their target audience. Here are three major factors influencing consumer behavior:

1. Psychological Factors: Consumer behavior is influenced by various psychological factors, such as perception, motivation, attitude, and learning. Perception involves how consumers perceive products and brands based on their senses. Motivation refers to the needs and desires that drive consumer behavior, while attitude encompasses the individual's beliefs, opinions, and evaluations of a particular product or brand. Learning refers to the process by which consumers acquire knowledge and modify their behavior based on past experiences.

2. Social Factors: Social factors like family, friends, and society can significantly influence consumer behavior. Consumer purchase decisions may be influenced by family members who act as decision-makers or opinion leaders. Reference groups, which are groups with whom individuals identify, can also shape their preferences and purchasing decisions. Moreover, societal

factors like culture, social class, and subculture can affect consumers' buying behavior depending on their values, norms, and beliefs.

3. Situational Factors: Consumer behavior can also be influenced by various situational factors, including the physical environment, time, and urgency. The physical environment, such as store layout or product display, can influence purchase decisions by creating positive or negative associations. Time factors like the availability of time, urgency, or seasonality can also impact consumer behavior. Urgent needs or limited-time offers can increase consumer motivation to make immediate purchases.

In conclusion, understanding market trends and consumer behavior is crucial for businesses to adapt to changing market dynamics and gain a competitive edge. By analyzing current market trends such as digital transformation, sustainability, and personalization, businesses can adapt their strategies to meet consumer expectations. Additionally, understanding psychological, social, and situational factors can help businesses comprehend and respond effectively to consumer behavior, leading to enhanced customer experiences and increased chances of success.

Chapter 4: Food Technology and Smart Kitchens

In recent years, the food industry has seen a significant transformation with the integration of technology into various aspects of the food preparation process. This chapter delves into the world of food technology and smart kitchens, exploring the advancements that have revolutionized how we cook, store, and consume food. From innovative gadgets to intelligent appliances, the integration of technology has brought about numerous benefits, making our lives in the kitchen more convenient, efficient, and eco-friendly.

1. Smart Appliances:

Smart appliances have become a game-changer in the kitchen, fundamentally changing the way we interact with our cooking devices. These technologically advanced appliances possess features that enable automated cooking, personalized recipes, and remote control capabilities. For instance, smart ovens can analyze the type and quantity of food placed inside, adjust temperature and cooking time accordingly, and provide notifications through smartphone apps. Similarly, smart refrigerators utilize sensors to monitor food inventory, suggest grocery items to purchase, and even prioritize items based on expiry dates, reducing food wastage.

2. Improved Cooking Techniques:

Food technology has paved the way for innovative cooking techniques that were previously difficult or impossible to achieve. Techniques like sous vide cooking, which involves vacuum-sealing food and cooking it in a precisely controlled water bath, have gained popularity through the use of immersion circulators. This process allows for evenly cooked, tender, and succulent dishes that elevate the overall taste and texture. Other techniques, such as pressure cooking, air frying, and steam baking, have also been simplified and made more accessible through technology, enabling individuals to experiment with diverse culinary styles.

3. Smart Kitchen Gadgets:

The rise of smart kitchen gadgets has heralded a new era of connectivity between appliances and users. Ranging from smart scales, which accurately measure ingredients and provide nutritional information, to smart coffee makers, which can be controlled via voice commands or smartphone applications, these gadgets streamline cooking processes and add convenience to everyday culinary experiences. Moreover, smart gadgets like herb gardens with automated watering systems, indoor grills with smoke extraction capabilities, and intelligent utensils that analyze food composition offer users unparalleled convenience and freedom in the kitchen.

4. Sustainability:

Food technology has also contributed to the promotion of sustainable practices in the kitchen. Smart kitchens allow for precise temperature control, reducing energy wastage, while connected appliances can monitor energy consumption and suggest energy-efficient cooking methods. Furthermore, various smart systems monitor water usage and ensure optimum utilization in tasks such as steam cooking or cleaning. Additionally, smart packaging solutions, such as vacuum sealers, extend the shelf life of food and reduce the need for preservatives, promoting both environmental conservation and minimal food wastage.

FOOD TECHNOLOGY AND smart kitchens have unleashed a wave of innovation in the culinary world, offering endless possibilities and transforming our culinary experiences. From smart appliances that automate cooking processes to gadgets that simplify meal preparation, these technologies have revolutionized the way we cook and consume food, making our lives easier, diverse, and sustainable. Embracing these advancements can unlock new levels of creativity and efficiency in the kitchen, enabling us to explore the vast and exciting world of gastronomy like never before.

Food technology has come a long way in recent years, with advancements in various areas of food production and preservation. These advancements have not only revolutionized the way we produce and consume food but have also addressed important issues such as food waste, nutritional content, and sustainability.

One of the most significant advancements in food technology is the development of genetically modified organisms (GMOs). GMOs are created by manipulating the DNA of plants and animals to enhance certain desirable traits, such as pest resistance and higher nutritional content. This technology has allowed farmers to grow crops that are more resistant to diseases and pests, resulting in increased productivity and reduced reliance on chemical pesticides.

Another area where food technology has made significant advancements is food preservation. Long gone are the days when preserving food meant pickling or canning. Today, we have techniques such as freeze-drying, which involves removing moisture from food to increase its shelf life without the need for additives or preservatives. This technology has not only improved the quality and taste of preserved food but has also led to the development of convenient freeze-dried meals for backpackers and astronauts.

Moreover, advances in food processing technology have allowed for the creation of various functional foods. These foods are fortified with additional nutrients and ingredients to target specific health needs. For example, we now have enriched milk products that provide additional calcium and vitamin D, helping to combat deficiencies and promote bone health. Functional foods have opened up new possibilities for improving our diet and addressing nutritional gaps in a fast-paced world.

In recent years, there has been a growing emphasis on sustainable food production and reducing food waste. Food technology has played a vital role in achieving these goals. For instance, advancements in packaging technology have led to the development of smart packaging materials that can detect and indicate food spoilage, reducing waste and improving food safety. Similarly, the use of novel preservation techniques such as high-pressure processing and pulsed electric fields has extended the shelf life of perishable foods, minimizing waste and reducing the demand for chemical preservatives.

Lastly, advancements in food technology have also revolutionized the way we consume and enjoy food. The rise of food delivery apps and meal kit services makes it easier than ever to access a wide range of cuisines and flavors from the comfort of our homes. Food technology has enabled more efficient supply chains and improved food safety measures, ensuring that consumers have access to diverse and safe food options.

In conclusion, advancements in food technology have brought about numerous benefits that are transforming the food industry. From GMOs to functional foods and sustainable production methods, technology has revolutionized the way we produce, preserve, and consume food. As our understanding of food science continues to expand, we can expect even more exciting advancements in the future, shaping the way we eat and nourish ourselves.

The advent of smart kitchen gadgets has truly revolutionized the way we cook and prepare our meals. Gone are the days of laboring for hours over a hot stove, only to be left with a mediocre dish. With the help of these cutting-edge appliances, anyone can become a master chef in their own kitchen.

One such gadget that has gained immense popularity in recent years is the smart kitchen thermometer. This device takes the guesswork out of cooking meat and ensures perfectly cooked dishes every time. Simply insert the probe into the meat, connect it to your smartphone, and monitor the internal temperature in real-time. The accompanying app even provides recommendations for achieving different levels of doneness, allowing you to customize your meals to your preferred taste.

Another game-changer in the realm of smart kitchen gadgets is the intelligent oven. These high-tech ovens are equipped with multiple sensors that regulate temperature and humidity throughout the cooking process, ensuring even heating and optimal results. With the ability to connect to your smartphone or tablet, you can remotely control and monitor the oven, receiving notifications when your dish is done or if any adjustments need to be made.

Smart coffee makers have also made their mark in the kitchen gadget industry. Imagine waking up to the enticing aroma of freshly brewed coffee, without even having to get out of bed. With a smart coffee maker, you can program your ideal brewing settings from your smartphone and have a perfect cup of joe waiting for you as soon as you enter the kitchen. Some models even offer the convenience of ordering coffee beans or pods directly, so you never have to worry about running out of your favorite blend.

The evolution of smart kitchen gadgets doesn't stop at food preparation alone. Even the mundane task of washing dishes has seen dramatic advancements. Smart dishwashers are equipped with sensors that detect the level of dirt on each dish, adjusting the water pressure and temperature accordingly. Additionally, they can be controlled remotely, allowing you to start or schedule a wash cycle from anywhere in your home.

Beyond the convenience factor, smart kitchen gadgets also contribute to a more sustainable lifestyle. Many of these devices are designed to save energy by utilizing advanced sensors and algorithms to optimize cooking times and reduce power consumption. They can also provide valuable insights into your cooking habits, helping you become more efficient and minimize waste.

In conclusion, the emergence of smart kitchen gadgets has transformed the way we approach cooking and meal preparation. From precise temperature control to automated brewing processes, these devices have truly streamlined and enhanced our culinary experiences. Whether you're a beginner in the kitchen or a seasoned chef, the advent of smart kitchen gadgets is sure to revolutionize your cooking game.

The impact of technology on food preparation and safety has been significant in recent years. Advances in technology have not only made cooking more convenient and efficient but have also increased the safety of food preparation processes.

One of the major impacts of technology on food preparation is the introduction of various kitchen appliances that have simplified and accelerated the cooking process. For example, the microwave oven has revolutionized the way food is heated up, allowing for quick, easy, and even cooking. This has not only saved time but has also ensured that food is evenly cooked and free from harmful bacteria.

Another important technological advancement in food preparation is the development of electric appliances like blenders, food processors, and mixers. These devices have made it easier to chop, grind, and blend ingredients, reducing the amount of manual labor required. This has not only made cooking more efficient but has also decreased the risk of contamination from handling food with unwashed hands.

Furthermore, the introduction of smart cooking devices has greatly impacted food safety. These devices are equipped with sensors and timers that monitor cooking temperatures and times, ensuring that food is cooked thoroughly and to the appropriate temperature. This is particularly important for meats and poultry, as undercooked food can lead to foodborne illnesses.

Additionally, these smart devices often come with built-in safety features such as automatic shut-off, preventing potential kitchen mishaps.

Besides cooking appliances, technology has also revolutionized food safety management systems. With advancements in computer technology and the internet, it has become easier for food businesses to track and monitor the safety of their products. For instance, some restaurants use digital thermometers that automatically store temperature data, making it easier to comply with food safety regulations and identify potential hazards.

Moreover, the development of food safety apps and online resources has empowered individuals to better understand and practice safe food handling techniques. These apps provide information on storage temperatures, expiry dates, and safe food handling practices, ensuring that consumers are well-informed about food safety.

In conclusion, technology has had a significant impact on food preparation and safety. From the introduction of convenient kitchen appliances to smart cooking devices and improved food safety management systems, technology has made cooking easier, efficient, and safer. Furthermore, the availability of food safety apps and online resources has empowered individuals to take charge of their own food safety, leading to healthier and safer eating practices.

4.4. Future Trends in Kitchen Tech

The rapid advancement in technology has opened up a world of possibilities, not only transforming our way of life but also revolutionizing the heart of every home - the kitchen. Kitchen tech has come a long way from simple appliances to interconnected smart devices that enhance convenience, efficiency, and safety. However, the future holds even more exciting prospects for kitchen tech that will shape the way we cook, eat, and live in our homes.

One of the most notable future trends in kitchen tech is the advent of smart appliances. We are already familiar with refrigerators that can tell us when we're running low on groceries, but the future holds appliances that can even order groceries automatically based on our consumption patterns. Imagine opening your fridge to find it fully stocked with all your favorite items. This technology will not only save time and effort but will also ensure we never run out of essential ingredients.

Another exciting trend is the integration of artificial intelligence (AI) in kitchen tech. AI-powered virtual assistants, such as Amazon Alexa or Google

Assistant, have become commonplace, but their potential for the kitchen is immense. Imagine having a virtual chef that recommends recipes based on the ingredients in your pantry, assists you in executing complex cooking techniques, and adjusts cooking times and temperatures for optimized results. AI will elevate our cooking skills and inspire culinary creativity like never before.

As we become more conscious of our health and environmental impact, advancements in kitchen tech will support these efforts in innovative ways. Precision nutrition tools will become commonplace, with kitchen scales that can analyze the nutritional content of our food. These smart scales will provide real-time feedback on the calorie, fat, protein, and carbohydrate content, enabling us to make informed choices about our diets. Additionally, kitchen appliances and gadgets will focus on energy efficiency and waste reduction, helping us lead more sustainable lifestyles.

Another trend worth noting is the rise of personalized cooking experiences. With the help of technology, we will be able to tailor recipes and ingredient quantities to our specific dietary preferences and restrictions. Smart cooktops and ovens will automatically adjust cooking times and temperatures for different diet plans, such as vegan, gluten-free, or keto. These advancements will make cooking accessible and enjoyable for everyone, irrespective of dietary requirements.

Furthermore, kitchen tech will also take advantage of the Internet of Things (IoT) concept. Connected kitchen devices will seamlessly communicate with one another, making cooking a seamless and coordinated experience. For example, imagine a scenario where your smart refrigerator communicates with your smart oven to preheat at the precise moment your dish is ready for baking. The IoT will enhance efficiency, reduce human errors, and revolutionize the way we interact with our kitchen appliances.

In conclusion, the future of kitchen tech holds immense potential for transforming our cooking experiences. Smart appliances, AI integration, personalized cooking, nutritional analysis, sustainability, and IoT connectivity are just a few of the trends that will shape our kitchens in the years to come. As technology continues to evolve, our kitchens will become intelligent, intuitive, and supportive partners in our culinary adventures, ultimately enhancing our quality of life. So, get ready to embrace the future of kitchen tech and prepare for an exciting journey in the world of delicious possibilities!

Chapter 5: Urban Farming and Sustainability

In recent years, a growing concern for the environment and the need for sustainable practices has led to the rise of urban farming. Urban farming is an innovative solution to address food security, reduce waste, and promote a greener and healthier lifestyle. This chapter will delve into the world of urban farming, exploring its benefits, techniques, and its significance in building a sustainable future.

Section 1: Understanding Urban Farming

1.1 What is Urban Farming?

- Introduction to the concept of urban farming and its basic principles.

- Highlighting the difference between traditional and urban agriculture.

- Exploring the range of urban farming activities, including rooftop gardens, vertical farming, and community gardens.

1.2 The Benefits of Urban Farming

- Examining the environmental advantages, including carbon footprint reduction and air quality improvement.

- Discussing the social and economic benefits of urban farming, such as food security and job creation.

- Exploring the health benefits of locally grown and organic produce.

Section 2: Techniques in Urban Farming

2.1 Hydroponics: Growing Without Soil

- Explaining the principles of hydroponics and how it can be utilized in urban farming.

- Discussing the advantages of hydroponics, such as water and space efficiency.

- Highlighting successful examples of hydroponic systems in urban environments.

2.2 Aquaponics: A Symbiotic System

- Introduction to aquaponics and how it combines fish farming with plant cultivation.

- Exploring the benefits of this closed-loop system, including nutrient recycling and reduced water consumption.

- Discussing the challenges and opportunities for implementing aquaponic systems in urban areas.

2.3 Vertical Farming: Reimagining Agricultural Spaces

- Exploring the concept of vertical farming and vertical gardens in urban settings.

- Examining the advantages of vertical farming, such as maximized space utilization and year-round crop production.

- Discussing the technological advancements in vertical farming and their potential impact on sustainability.

Section 3: Promoting Urban Farming and Sustainability

3.1 Urban Farming Policies and Initiatives

- Analyzing the role of local governments and organizations in promoting urban farming.

- Highlighting successful urban farming initiatives from various cities around the world.

- Discussing the challenges and opportunities in improving urban farming policies.

3.2 Education and Outreach Programs

- Emphasizing the importance of educating communities about urban farming practices.

- Discussing the role of educational institutions and non-profit organizations in providing training and awareness programs.

- Examining the impact of community involvement and the empowerment of individuals through urban farming.

URBAN FARMING HAS BECOME an essential component of sustainable urban development. Its benefits are multifaceted, with the potential to address societal, environmental, and economic challenges. By implementing innovative techniques and educating communities, urban farming has the power to transform urban landscapes into vibrant and resilient ecosystems, ensuring a more sustainable future for generations to come.

Over the past few decades, there has been a growing trend towards urban farming. People living in cities have started to recognize the benefits of growing their own food and taking charge of their own food security. This urban farming revolution is transforming the way we look at cities and agriculture.

Urban farming can take many forms, from rooftop gardens to community gardens to hydroponic systems in empty warehouses. No matter the scale or design, the goal remains the same – to grow fresh, nutritious food in urban environments. This not only provides a source of food for urban dwellers but also has a multitude of other benefits.

One of the most significant advantages of urban farming is the reduction of food miles. In traditional food systems, food travels on average 1,500 miles before reaching the consumer's plate. This not only results in high carbon emissions but also compromises the quality and freshness of the food. Urban farming cuts down on food miles as produce is grown closer to where it is consumed, ensuring that it reaches consumers at the peak of its freshness and nutritional value.

Moreover, urban farming contributes to the creation of green spaces in cities. Concrete jungles are often devoid of plants and greenery, leading to a lack of biodiversity and negative impacts on mental well-being. Urban farming reintroduces plants and green spaces into cities, providing habitat for birds, insects, and other organisms. It also enhances the air quality by absorbing carbon dioxide and releasing oxygen. Additionally, the presence of urban farms can improve the aesthetic appeal of neighborhoods, creating a sense of community pride and fostering stronger social connections.

Another key benefit of urban farming is its potential to address food access and food justice issues. Many urban areas suffer from limited access to fresh, healthy food, also known as food deserts. Urban farms can act as community food hubs, providing residents with access to affordable, locally grown produce. They can also be used to educate and empower communities about sustainable and healthy food choices.

Furthermore, urban farming can play a significant role in sustainable waste management. Food waste is a major issue in urban areas, with a significant portion of the waste going to landfills. Urban farms can utilize organic waste to produce compost, which can be used as a natural fertilizer for crops. This practice not only reduces waste but also helps maintain soil health and promotes sustainable agriculture.

While the benefits of urban farming are plentiful, it is not without its challenges. Limited space and high land prices in urban areas can make it difficult for individuals or communities to start or expand urban farms. Availability of water and suitable infrastructure are also essential for successful urban farming operations. Additionally, urban farmers face unique challenges such as pollution, pests, and the need for proper waste management systems. However, these challenges can be overcome through innovative strategies and government support.

The urban farming revolution holds tremendous promise for transforming our cities into sustainable, resilient, and healthy environments. By reconnecting people with their food sources and creating greener urban landscapes, urban farming has the potential to improve the well-being of both individuals and communities. As the movement gains momentum, it is essential for governments, organizations, and individuals to recognize and support the value of urban farming in creating a healthier and more sustainable future.

Urban agriculture refers to the practice of cultivating and producing food within urban areas. As cities continue to expand and resources become increasingly limited, urban agriculture has gained significant attention as a sustainable solution to food security, environmental sustainability, and community engagement. Various techniques and technologies have been developed to maximize the efficiency and productivity of urban agriculture.

1. Vertical farming: One of the primary challenges of urban agriculture is limited space. Vertical farming offers a solution by growing plants in vertically stacked layers instead of traditional horizontal fields. This technique utilizes hydroponics or aeroponics systems, where plants are grown in a nutrient-rich water solution or in air with nutrient mist. Vertical farming reduces the need for land and minimizes water usage, offering higher yields in a smaller area.

2. Aquaponics: Aquaponics is a combination of aquaculture (fish farming) and hydroponics. In an aquaponics system, waste produced by fish is used as a nutrient source for plants grown hydroponically. Plants, in turn, purify the water before it is recirculated back to the fish tanks. This closed-loop system is highly sustainable, as it requires less water and eliminates the need for chemical

fertilizers. Aquaponics could be integrated into urban spaces like rooftops, providing fresh produce and fish within a dense cityscape.

3. Controlled environment agriculture: Most urban areas lack favorable climatic conditions for year-round agricultural production. However, the controlled environment agriculture (CEA) technique enables crops to be grown within a controlled environment, irrespective of external weather conditions. CEA incorporates technologies such as greenhouses, vertical farms, and indoor farming to maintain optimal temperature, humidity, light, and nutrient levels for plant growth. These conditions help maximize crop yields and extend growing seasons, allowing urban farmers to produce food throughout the year.

4. Rooftop gardens: With limited access to land, rooftops offer a viable space for urban agriculture. Rooftop gardens involve transforming the top of buildings into green spaces for growing food crops. These gardens utilize various techniques such as container gardening, vertical farming, and hydroponics. Besides providing fresh food, rooftop gardens also enhance insulation, conserve energy, and contribute to urban biodiversity. They can be particularly effective in buildings with flat roofs or those designed to bear the weight of garden structures.

5. Community gardens: Urban agriculture is not solely focused on maximizing yields; it also seeks to promote community engagement and social integration. Community gardens are shared spaces where residents can cultivate their crops collectively. These gardens foster a sense of community, provide educational opportunities, and facilitate access to fresh produce for individuals who may not have the space or resources to grow their food. Community gardens can be established in public or private spaces, such as parks, vacant lots, or even on rooftops.

Numerous additional technologies and techniques are integrated into urban agriculture practices, such as rainwater harvesting, composting, rooftop greenhouse technologies, and the use of sensors for automated monitoring and irrigation. Furthermore, advancements in artificial intelligence, robotics, and precision agriculture are being researched for their potential integration into urban agriculture in the future.

In conclusion, urban agriculture presents a sustainable and productive solution to address food scarcity in urban areas. Techniques and technologies designed for urban agriculture, including vertical farming, aquaponics, controlled environment agriculture, rooftop gardens, and community gardens, enable efficient and environmentally friendly food production. The continuous exploration and adoption of innovative techniques and technologies hold great promise for the future of urban agriculture and our ability to produce fresh, local food within urban landscapes.

Urban Farms and Community Impact

Urban farming has become a popular trend in many cities around the world. This practice involves growing vegetables, fruits, and sometimes raising livestock in urban areas. The idea behind urban farming is to provide fresh, locally sourced food to urban residents and promote a sense of community.

One of the most significant impacts of urban farming is the increased accessibility to fresh food. In many urban areas, access to fresh produce is limited, with most residents relying heavily on heavily processed and packaged foods. Urban farms provide a solution to this problem by bringing healthy food options directly to the community.

Furthermore, urban farming promotes sustainability and reduces the carbon footprint. By growing food locally, resources such as water and energy are conserved. Transporting food over long distances contributes to pollution and greenhouse gas emissions. With urban farming, food can be grown and consumed within the city, reducing the need for transportation.

Urban farming also contributes to the revitalization of local communities. Abandoned lots and vacant buildings can be transformed into productive green spaces. These revitalized spaces create an aesthetically pleasing environment that promotes social interaction among residents. Urban farms become hubs for community engagement, providing opportunities for individuals to come together and work towards a common goal.

Moreover, many urban farms engage in educational programs, targeting both children and adults. These programs aim to teach people about the importance of fresh food and sustainable living. They often offer workshops on gardening, culinary skills, and nutrition. By educating individuals about these topics, urban farms empower community members to make healthier and more environmentally conscious choices.

Additionally, urban farming can have a positive economic impact on communities. It can create job opportunities for local residents, whether it be through farming, marketing, or distribution. Supporting local urban farms also promotes the growth of small businesses. Instead of relying on large, corporate food chains, urban residents can support their local farmers and contribute to the local economy.

In summary, urban farming has a wide range of impacts on communities. From increased accessibility to fresh food, to the promotion of sustainability and community engagement, urban farms play a vital role in transforming urban landscapes. This practice simultaneously addresses issues such as food security, environmental sustainability, and community well-being. As urban areas continue to grow and face various challenges, urban farming will likely continue to be a relevant and important solution.

Title: Case Studies in Successful Urban Farming: Exemplary Models of Sustainable Agriculture in Cities

URBAN FARMING IS AN emerging phenomenon that seeks to bring sustainable agriculture into densely populated cities. The practice has gained significant attention in recent years due to its potential to address food security, promote sustainability, and foster community engagement. This article aims to explore five remarkable case studies that demonstrate successful urban farming initiatives in various parts of the world. These exemplary models provide valuable insights into the socio-economic, environmental, and health benefits associated with urban farming. By delving into the key factors behind these success stories, we can uncover invaluable lessons and inspiration for future urban farming projects.

1. Brooklyn Grange, New York, USA:

Brooklyn Grange, located on rooftop spaces in New York City, is one of the largest rooftop farms in the world. By converting unutilized buildings into thriving agricultural spaces, Brooklyn Grange allows city dwellers to have access to locally grown, fresh produce. With its focus on organic farming practices, the farm not only provides hyper-local food options but also reduces the carbon footprint associated with food transportation.

2. The Vertical Farm, Singapore:

Singapore, known for its limited land space, has embraced vertical farming as a solution to domestic food production. The Vertical Farm, located within a skyscraper, maximizes agricultural output by utilizing a combination of hydroponics and vertical farming techniques. By growing vegetables using soil-less methods in vertically stacked layers, the farm produces higher yields while conserving water and reducing the need for chemical pesticides.

3. Growing Power's Allen Urban Farm, Wisconsin, USA:

Located in Milwaukee, Wisconsin, Growing Power's Allen Urban Farm is a beacon of sustainability and community involvement. The farm operates year-round, providing a diverse range of crops, fish, and livestock within an economically disadvantaged neighborhood. By integrating renewable energy systems, aquaponics, and vermiculture, Growing Power demonstrates the potential of urban farming to address both food security and socio-economic disparities.

4. Kompot, Moscow, Russia:

At Kompot, an urban farm situated in Moscow, Russia, the focus is primarily on agroforestry and permaculture principles. By combining fruit trees, bushes, and herbs with eco-friendly agricultural practices, Kompot creates an integrated and biodiverse ecosystem. By promoting biodiversity, Kompot fosters a healthier urban environment while offering fresh, nutritious produce to city residents.

5. Ta'riqa Gardens, Cape Town, South Africa:

South Africa's Ta'riqa Gardens showcases how urban farming can empower marginalized communities. Located within an impoverished area of Cape Town, this urban farm prioritizes community development, job creation, and sustainable food production. Their focus on education and training enables individuals to gain agricultural skills, boosting both self-sufficiency and economic empowerment.

THESE CASE STUDIES in successful urban farming highlight diverse approaches to sustainable agriculture within urban settings. While each project differs in scope and focus, their common thread lies in addressing food security, environmental sustainability, and community engagement. These initiatives prove that urban farming is not merely a trend but a tangible solution to numerous challenges faced by modern cities. By drawing upon the lessons and experiences gained from these successful endeavors, policymakers and urban developers can leverage the power of urban farming to build resilient, healthy, and sustainable cities of tomorrow.

Chapter 6: Fusion Cuisine – Blending Borders

In recent years, there has been a growing interest in fusion cuisine, which combines elements from different culinary traditions to create unique and flavorful dishes. Fusion cuisine reflects the continually evolving nature of food and the way cultural influences shape our palates. This chapter explores the fascinating world of fusion cuisine, its origins, and its impact on modern gastronomy.

1. Exploring Fusion Cuisine

Fusion cuisine, as the name suggests, involves the blending of culinary traditions and ingredients from different cultures. By merging elements from diverse gastronomic traditions, chefs create innovative dishes that showcase the best of each culture while fostering a harmonious culinary experience. Fusion cuisine not only pays tribute to various cuisines but also introduces new flavors and techniques.

2. The Origins of Fusion Cuisine

Though fusion cuisine today is often associated with contemporary culinary trends, its roots can be traced back centuries. For example, the culinary fusion between Indian and Persian cuisines led to the creation of Mughlai cuisine in India. Mughlai dishes exemplify a unique blend of Persian spices and Indian cooking techniques. Similarly, the Portuguese influence on Japanese cuisine resulted in the birth of fusion dishes like tempura.

3. The Rise of Fusion Cuisine in Modern Times

In recent decades, the globalization of food and the increased accessibility of ingredients from different cultures have contributed to the popularity of fusion cuisine. Chefs today have the liberty to experiment with a wide range of ingredients, drawing inspiration from multiple culinary traditions to create exciting, boundary-pushing dishes. This culinary trend has not only expanded the choices available to diners but has also challenged traditional notions of cooking and encouraged creativity in the kitchen.

4. Blending Borders: Examples of Fusion Cuisine

Fusion cuisine knows no bounds, and chefs worldwide constantly push the envelope when it comes to merging flavors and cultural influences. One popular example of fusion cuisine is the combination of Japanese and Peruvian culinary traditions, known as Nikkei cuisine. Nikkei dishes blend traditional Japanese ingredients and techniques with Peruvian flavors, resulting in innovative dishes such as tiradito, a sashimi-like dish with Peruvian-inspired sauces.

Another notable example is the fusion of Mexican and Korean cuisines, aptly called Korean-Mexican fusion. This inventive blend combines Korean barbecue techniques with traditional Mexican ingredients like tacos and quesadillas, giving birth to mouthwatering creations such as Korean bulgogi tacos.

5. The Impact of Fusion Cuisine on Culinary Traditions

The rise of fusion cuisine has had a profound impact on culinary traditions worldwide. As chefs experiment with new flavors and techniques, they contribute to the evolution of traditional cuisines, while simultaneously creating new ones. Fusion cuisine encourages cultural exchange, fostering appreciation for the diversity of global gastronomy and breaking down cultural barriers through shared culinary experiences.

Conclusion

Fusion cuisine stands as a testament to the ever-changing and dynamic nature of food. Through blending borders and merging culinary traditions, chefs create dishes that reflect the evolution of gastronomy, challenging our tastes and expanding our palates. With its ability to foster cultural exchange and appreciation worldwide, fusion cuisine facilitates a melting pot of flavors and paves the way for creativity and innovation in the kitchen.

Fusion cuisine is a term that has gained significant popularity and recognition in recent years, but its history goes back much further than one might expect. In order to fully appreciate and understand the concept of fusion cuisine, it is important to take a look at its historical perspectives and origins.

The concept of fusion cuisine can be traced back to ancient times, where global trade and cultural exchange played a significant role in the development of culinary practices. One notable example is the Silk Road, an ancient network of trade routes that connected various regions of the world, including Asia,

Africa, and Europe. The Silk Road facilitated the exchange of goods, ideas, and, of course, food. As different cultures came into contact with one another, they began to adopt and adapt aspects of each other's cuisine, resulting in the creation of unique fusion dishes.

A prime example of fusion cuisine can be seen in the culinary traditions of Southeast Asia. The region's cuisine is an amalgamation of flavors and techniques from various cultures, including Indian, Chinese, and European influences. For instance, dishes like the Nasi Goreng from Indonesia, which is a fried rice dish made with Indonesian spices and condiments, are a result of the fusion of Chinese and Indonesian cooking methods.

In more recent history, fusion cuisine began to gain significant attention and recognition during the late 20th and early 21st centuries. This was partly due to the increasing interest in global travel and cultural exchange, which exposed individuals to a variety of culinary traditions. This exposure led to chefs and food enthusiasts experimenting with blending different flavors, ingredients, and cooking techniques to create innovative and unique dishes.

Chefs like Wolfgang Puck and Nobu Matsuhisa played a crucial role in popularizing fusion cuisine during this period. Puck, an Austrian-born American chef, introduced a fusion of European and Asian flavors in his dishes, combining ingredients and techniques from both traditions. Meanwhile, Matsuhisa, a Japanese chef, showcased the fusion of traditional Japanese cuisine with influences from Latin America and other regions, resulting in his signature style of Japanese-Peruvian fusion.

The rise of fusion cuisine also coincided with the growing appreciation for locally sourced ingredients and the farm-to-table movement. Chefs started incorporating local, seasonal produce and artisanal products into their fusion dishes, further adding depth and complexity to their creations.

Today, fusion cuisine has become deeply ingrained in the culinary landscape, with chefs and home cooks continuing to experiment with different combinations of flavors, ingredients, and techniques. The concept of fusion cuisine allows individuals to explore and celebrate the diversity of culinary traditions from all over the world, creating exciting and enticing dishes that showcase a blend of cultural influences.

In conclusion, the historical perspectives on fusion cuisine can be traced back to ancient trade routes and cultural exchange, where blending different culinary practices resulted in the creation of unique fusion dishes. The concept gained significant recognition in recent history, with chefs like Wolfgang Puck and Nobu Matsuhisa pioneering the fusion of flavors and techniques from diverse culinary traditions. Today, fusion cuisine continues to evolve and thrive, serving as a beautiful reflection of cultural diversity and culinary creativity.

In the modern era, fusion cuisine has emerged as an exciting culinary trend that seamlessly blends together different food traditions and ingredients from all around the world. This unique style of cooking has gained popularity due to its ability to create innovative, flavorful, and unexpected dishes that tantalize the taste buds. Fusion cuisine encourages chefs to think outside the box and experiment with new flavors and techniques, resulting in a melting pot of cuisines that can be found in restaurants and households worldwide.

What sets fusion cuisine apart from traditional cuisine is its fearless combination of different ingredients and tastes. Chefs are no longer bound by the constraints of sticking to one specific culinary tradition. Instead, they are encouraged to let their creativity soar by incorporating elements from multiple sources. For example, a dish may feature a combination of Italian pasta with a spicy Thai sauce, or Japanese sushi topped with Mexican salsa. The possibilities are endless, and it is this sense of adventure and surprise that makes fusion cuisine so appealing to food enthusiasts.

Fusion cuisine has its roots in a long history of culinary exchange and cross-cultural influences. Throughout the years, people have traveled and migrated, bringing with them their food traditions and ingredients, as well as adapting to their new surroundings. This exchange of ideas and ingredients has contributed to the formation of fusion cuisine as we know it today. For instance, the fusion of Asian flavors with French cooking techniques, known as Asian-French fusion, resulted in popular dishes such as Vietnamese pho with foie gras or Chinese dumplings with truffle-infused fillings.

One of the reasons why fusion cuisine resonates so strongly with people is its ability to represent the multicultural nature of our society. Fusion dishes not only symbolize diversity and inclusion but also play a role in fostering cultural understanding. By blending different ingredients and techniques, fusion cuisine celebrates and pays homage to a variety of culinary traditions, giving them a platform to shine and be appreciated by a wider audience.

Moreover, fusion cuisine has become a culinary playground for chefs to showcase their skills and creativity. It challenges them to think critically and imaginatively about flavor combinations, presentation, and even the dining experience itself. The fusion of global cuisines inspires chefs to experiment with new ingredients and techniques, pushing the boundaries of traditional cooking and culinary concepts.

One notable trend within fusion cuisine is the experimentation with plant-based and alternative proteins. The rise of vegetarian, vegan, and flexitarian diets has sparked an interest in creating dishes that combine various vegetarian and traditional meat-based traditions. For instance, plant-based sushi rolls using tempeh or seitan as the main protein, or vegetable stir-fries with plant-based seafood alternatives like jackfruit. These creative combinations highlight the growing demand for sustainable and ethical dining experiences.

In conclusion, fusion cuisine in the modern era represents an exciting melding of culinary traditions and flavors. It challenges chefs to explore new avenues of taste and incorporates multicultural influences into their dishes. Whether it be by blending Italian and Thai flavors or fusing techniques from Asian and French cuisine, fusion cuisine continues to captivate food enthusiasts and highlight the richness and diversity of our culinary world.

In this section, we will dive into the world of fusion cuisine and explore some notable fusion restaurants that have made their mark in the industry. Fusion restaurants are known for their innovative and often surprising blends of different culinary traditions, resulting in unique and exciting flavor combinations.

1. Nobu (Japanese-Peruvian Fusion):

Nobu, founded by Chef Nobu Matsuhisa in the late 1980s, is considered one of the pioneers of fusion cuisine. With a focus on blending traditional Japanese dishes with Peruvian ingredients and flavors, Nobu has created a distinctive culinary experience. Some of their iconic dishes include Nobu-style sashimi with jalapeno, black cod miso, and sake-infused tiramisu.

2. Momofuku (Asian Cuisine with a Twist):

Founded by Korean-American chef David Chang in 2004, Momofuku has garnered a cult following for its inventive takes on Asian cuisine. From their pork belly buns to kimchi fried rice, Momofuku infuses traditional Asian flavors with unexpected ingredients and techniques. With multiple locations globally, Momofuku has become a household name in the fusion restaurant scene.

3. Chifa (Chinese-Peruvian Fusion):

Originating in Peru, Chifa is the fusion of Chinese and Peruvian cuisines. With a rich history influenced by Chinese immigrants to Peru, Chifa restaurants offer a unique blend of techniques and ingredients. Dishes like lomo saltado (stir-fried beef), chaufa (Chinese-style fried rice), and causa rellena (potato stuffed with meat or seafood) are staples in Chifa cuisine.

4. Gjelina (Mediterranean-California Fusion):

Located in Venice Beach, California, Gjelina is known for its farm-to-table approach and its fusion of Mediterranean and California cuisines. Their menu features dishes like blistered green beans with crispy garlic, wood-roasted branzino with salsa verde, and farro salad with roasted vegetables. By combining local produce and Mediterranean flavors, Gjelina offers a fresh and vibrant dining experience.

5. Blackbird (American-Mediterranean Fusion):

Based in Chicago, Blackbird showcases an innovative blend of American and Mediterranean flavors. With a focus on seasonal and locally-sourced ingredients, they offer dishes like roast lamb neck with confit potatoes, pork belly with mustard greens and cider gel, and sea scallops with sunchoke and pork sausage. The fusion of these two culinary traditions creates a menu that is creative, diverse, and constantly evolving.

6. Senia (Hawaiian-Contemporary Fusion):

Situated in Honolulu, Senia reflects the unique culinary heritage of Hawaii. By incorporating traditional Hawaiian ingredients and techniques, along with modern cooking approaches, Senia offers a new perspective on local cuisine. Dishes like uni toast with whipped lardo, Kauai prawns with miso eggplant, and smoked butter mochi showcase the creativity and artistry behind this Hawaiian-contemporary fusion restaurant.

In conclusion, these noteworthy fusion restaurants have successfully pushed culinary boundaries, offering diners a taste of innovative flavor combinations from around the world. Through a blend of different traditions and techniques, fusion cuisine continues to stimulate our palates and challenge our perceptions of food. Whether it's Japanese-Peruvian, Asian with a twist, or

Mediterranean-California fusion, these restaurants exemplify the diversity and excitement within the fusion restaurant scene.

In the world of culinary arts, fusion cuisine is a term that has gained popularity in recent years. It refers to the combining of various elements from different culinary traditions or regions to create dishes that have unique, often unexpected flavors. Fusion cuisine has been praised for its innovative and creative approach to cooking, but it also raises important questions about cultural implications and critiques.

One of the fascinating aspects of fusion cuisine is how it reflects the social and cultural changes that occur when different communities come into contact with each other. Many fusion dishes are the result of immigrants or travelers bringing their culinary traditions to new places and adapting them to local ingredients and tastes. This process can lead to exciting results, as it allows for the sharing and blending of culinary knowledge, traditions, and ingredients.

However, fusion cuisine is not without its critics. Some argue that it appropriates and commodifies traditional cuisines. For example, when a popular celebrity chef takes an ingredient or cooking technique from a particular culture and presents it as their own invention, it can be seen as exploitation or even cultural theft. Critics argue that this erases the historical and cultural significance of the cuisine, reduces it to a mere trendy fusion dish, and ignores the voices and contributions of the original creators.

Another criticism of fusion cuisine relates to power dynamics and gatekeeping. In the context of globalization and rising popularity of fusion dishes, culinary traditions from Western cultures often become dominant and overshadow the lesser-known or less valued cuisines from other regions. This can perpetuate unequal power structures in the global culinary landscape, where Western chefs and restaurants profit from incorporating elements from various cuisines, while the original contributors receive little recognition or compensation.

Furthermore, fusion cuisine can sometimes fall into the trap of oversimplification or cultural stereotypes. When chefs rely heavily on broad generalizations about a certain culture's cuisine, it can result in a distorted representation of that culture. By reducing culinary traditions to a few basic ingredients or techniques, fusion cuisine risks perpetuating misconceptions and perpetuating harmful stereotypes. It is crucial to approach fusion cuisine with a critical and respectful lens, appreciating the complexities and diversity of culinary cultures.

However, it is important to note that fusion cuisine can also serve as a way to bridge gaps between different cultures, fostering cross-cultural understanding, and appreciation. It can be a celebration of diversity and inclusivity, where various culinary traditions come together to create something entirely new and exciting. When done thoughtfully and with a deep understanding of the cultural roots involved, fusion cuisine has the potential to bring people together, break down barriers, and create a shared experience.

In conclusion, fusion cuisine is a phenomenon that has generated both interest and controversy within the culinary world. It offers a platform for creativity and innovation but must be approached with caution, considering the cultural implications and potential critiques. By respecting the origins of different culinary traditions, embracing diversity, and promoting meaningful cultural exchange, fusion cuisine can continue to push boundaries and contribute to the rich tapestry of global culinary heritage.

Chapter 7: Molecular Gastronomy – The Science of Cooking

THE CULINARY WORLD is constantly evolving, with new techniques and ingredients constantly being introduced to redefine the way we cook and eat. One such groundbreaking development is the emergence of molecular gastronomy, a field that fuses culinary arts with scientific principles to create innovative and intriguing dishes. In this chapter, we will delve into the world of molecular gastronomy and explore the fascinating science behind cooking.

1. The Birth of Molecular Gastronomy:

Molecular gastronomy first gained recognition in the late 1980s when Hervé This, a French physical chemist, brought the idea to the forefront. Collaborating with chefs such as Pierre Gagnaire and Ferran Adrià, This aimed to use scientific methods to understand and enhance traditional culinary techniques.

2. The Science behind Molecular Gastronomy:

a. Hydrocolloids: One of the key elements in molecular gastronomy is the utilization of hydrocolloids, which are substances that form gels when combined with liquid. These include agar-agar, xanthan gum, and carrageenan. Chefs can manipulate the texture of their dishes by employing hydrocolloids, creating unique textures like foams, gels, and pearls.

b. Sous Vide Cooking: By employing the technique of sous vide, meaning under vacuum, chefs carefully control the temperature at which their ingredients are cooked. This method preserves the natural flavors and textures while ensuring even cooking.

3. Spherification:

Spherification is a technique within molecular gastronomy that utilizes a gelling agent to create spheres with a liquid center. Chefs can transform liquid ingredients, such as fruit juices, into delicate and visually appealing spheres.

This technique has been widely popularized by the renowned chef Ferran Adrià, who initially experimented with spherification at his renowned restaurant, El Bulli.

4. Nitrogen and Culinary Creativity:

Liquid nitrogen has become an iconic tool in molecular gastronomy, thanks to its ability to rapidly freeze ingredients and create unique textures. The extreme cold temperature of liquid nitrogen allows chefs to make instant ice creams, freeze fruits, and even create smoky presentations. However, it requires careful handling to ensure safety.

5. Flavor Pairing:

Molecular gastronomy explores new possibilities for flavor pairing by considering the chemical compounds present in various ingredients. Chefs can create unexpected harmonies by combining ingredients that have complementary chemical profiles, leading to mind-boggling taste experiences.

6. The Role of Technology:

Molecular gastronomy heavily relies on cutting-edge technology to achieve its creative dishes. From centrifuges to rotary evaporators, advanced equipment allows chefs to extract pure flavors, transform textures, and unlock new culinary frontiers.

MOLECULAR GASTRONOMY stands as a bridge between cooking and science, exploring the realms of possibility within the culinary arts. Through the clever utilization of scientific principles and techniques, chefs can transform traditional recipes and ingredients into awe-inspiring culinary creations. By breaking down the barriers of tradition, molecular gastronomy pushes the boundaries of imagination and elevates the entire gastronomic experience.

Molecular gastronomy, a term coined in the 1980s, is gaining popularity in the culinary world as chefs seek to push the boundaries of traditional cooking and explore the science behind food.

In this introduction to molecular gastronomy, we will explore the origins of this culinary discipline, its key principles, and how it has revolutionized the field of gastronomy.

7.1.1 Origins of Molecular Gastronomy`

Molecular gastronomy found its beginnings in the vibrant city of Barcelona, Spain, during the late 1980s. This experimental approach to food emerged as a collaboration between physicist Nicholas Kurti and French chef Hervé This.

Both Kurti and This were fascinated by the scientific aspects of cooking and recognized the potential to elevate culinary creations using a deeper understanding of the chemical reactions that occur during the cooking process.

7.1.2 Key Principles of Molecular Gastronomy

At its core, molecular gastronomy seeks to merge culinary creativity with scientific knowledge to create innovative, visually stunning, and flavorful dishes. This uniquely interdisciplinary approach embraces the principles of chemistry and physics to understand and transform food on a molecular level.

Some of the key principles of molecular gastronomy include:

1. Understanding chemical reactions: Molecular gastronomy delves into the chemical reactions that occur when food is subjected to various cooking techniques, such as heating, cooling, and mixing. By studying these reactions, chefs can manipulate flavors, textures, and appearances.

2. Utilizing modern tools and technologies: Molecular gastronomy takes advantage of cutting-edge equipment and technologies such as sous vide cookers, rotary evaporators, and liquid nitrogen. These tools enable chefs to create innovative culinary masterpieces that would be otherwise unattainable.

3. Creating unique textures: Molecular gastronomy aims to challenge traditional cuisine by creating unique textures and mouthfeel in dishes. Chefs use techniques like spherification, gelification, and foams to play with textures and surprise diners' palates.

4. Exploring sensory perception: Molecular gastronomy redefines the dining experience by exploring various sensory perceptions such as taste, aroma, and presentation. By understanding the psychology behind food preferences and perception, chefs can create dishes that captivate all senses.

7.1.3. The Impact on Gastronomy

The emergence of molecular gastronomy has undoubtedly made a significant impact on the world of gastronomy. Chefs embracing this discipline have not only elevated the art of cooking but also stimulated dialogue and experimentation among culinary professionals.

This modern approach has led to innovative creations like edible food, flavored aerosols, and multi-textured dishes, revolutionizing the way we experience food. Molecular gastronomy has become a driving force for chefs to push boundaries, challenge norms, and transform the culinary landscape.

Moreover, it has opened up new avenues for collaborations between scientists, chefs, and food enthusiasts. This interdisciplinary approach fosters a culture of curiosity, exchange of knowledge, and continuous research and development, propelling culinary innovation to new heights.

In conclusion, molecular gastronomy is an exciting and evolving field that marries science and culinary artistry. With its strong foundation in chemical reactions, utilization of modern tools, emphasis on unique textures, and exploration of sensory perception, molecular gastronomy has broadened the horizons of the culinary world. As this discipline continues to evolve, chefs and scientists alike are continually pushing boundaries to create extraordinary dining experiences.

In this section, we will delve into the key techniques and ingredients used in various types of cooking and food preparation. These techniques and ingredients have been developed and perfected over time, resulting in distinct flavors, textures, and aromas that are unique to different cuisines around the world. From sautéing and simmering to marinating and grilling, let's explore some of these culinary techniques and learn about the ingredients that play a crucial role in creating delicious dishes.

1. Sautéing:

Sautéing is a cooking technique that involves quickly frying food in a small amount of fat over high heat. This technique is commonly used to cook vegetables, seafood, and meat. The high heat produces a caramelization effect on the surface of the food, adding flavors and creating a crispy texture. Common ingredients used in sautéing include garlic, onions, bell peppers, and various spices and herbs to enhance the flavors.

2. Simmering:

Simmering is a gentle cooking technique that involves cooking food in a liquid at a low, steady heat. It is often used for soups, stews, and sauces to infuse the flavors of the ingredients into the liquid. This slow method of cooking allows tough meats to become tender, and for the spices and herbs to blend seamlessly into the dish's overall taste. Common ingredients used in simmering include broth, wine, tomatoes, and a wide variety of vegetables and meats.

3. Marinating:

Marinating is the process of soaking food in a seasoned liquid or mixture to enhance its flavor and tenderness. This technique is commonly used for meat, poultry, and seafood, as it helps to impart flavors and tenderize the protein. The liquid used in marinating can contain various ingredients such as vinegar, citrus juice, oils, herbs, spices, and even yogurt. The marinating time can vary from a few minutes to several hours or even overnight, depending on the desired intensity of the flavors.

4. Grilling:

Grilling is a popular cooking technique that involves cooking food directly over an open flame or on a heated grill. It imparts a distinct smoky flavor and creates a charred exterior while maintaining the natural juices and tenderness of the food. Grilling is commonly used for meats, vegetables, and seafood. Ingredients used can range from marinated meats, brushed with sauces and spices, to seasoned vegetables and seafood seasoned with herbs and oils.

Now let's move on to key ingredients that are used in various culinary techniques:

1. Herbs and Spices:

Herbs and spices are crucial ingredients in many cuisines around the world. They not only provide flavor but also add aroma and depth to dishes. Common herbs include basil, rosemary, thyme, and cilantro, while common spices include cumin, paprika, turmeric, and cloves. Their use can vary depending on the regional cuisine and personal taste, making each dish unique and flavorful.

2. Dairy Products:

Dairy products such as milk, cheese, butter, and yogurt are staples in many cuisines. They are used in various forms, from enhancing flavors in sauces and desserts to providing creaminess and richness to dishes. Cheese is often melted or grated to add a creamy texture and savory flavor to pasta, while milk and yogurt can be used in soups, marinades, and baked goods.

3. Aromatics:

Aromatics refer to ingredients such as garlic, onions, and shallots that provide a strong aroma and flavor base in dishes. They are commonly used at the beginning of cooking processes, sautéed, or used to create a flavor base like a mirepoix or sofrito. Aromatics add depth and complexity to dishes through their unique flavor profiles.

4. Stocks and Broths:

Stocks and broths are flavorful liquids made by simmering vegetables, bones, and/or meat in water. They form the base of many soups, stews, and sauces, providing rich flavors and adding depth to dishes. Whether it's a vegetable stock, chicken broth, or beef stock, these flavorful liquids are essential in creating well-balanced and delicious meals.

These are just a few examples of key techniques and ingredients that play an important role in creating delicious dishes. The art of cooking is a combination of skill, creativity, and understanding the flavors, textures, and aromas that different techniques and ingredients bring to the table. By exploring different culinary techniques and experimenting with various ingredients, one can truly create unique and tasty creations in the kitchen.

Molecular gastronomy, often seen as a avant-garde culinary movement, has taken the culinary world by storm in recent years. Combining both science and art, molecular gastronomy aims to push the boundaries and explore the possibilities of food through experimentation with ingredients, textures, flavors, and presentation. While there has been an influx of innovative chefs embracing this technique, there are a few pioneers who have played a pivotal role in shaping the molecular gastronomy landscape. Here are some influential chefs who have had a significant impact on the field:

1. Ferran Adrià:

Often hailed as the father of molecular gastronomy, Ferran Adrià revolutionized the culinary world with his creativity and scientific approach in the kitchen. As the former head chef of the world-renowned El Bulli restaurant in Spain, Adrià pushed the boundaries of traditional cooking and experimented with ingredients like never before. He embraced techniques such as spherification, which transforms liquids into gel-like spheres, and played with innovative ways of incorporating foams, emulsions, and gels in his dishes. Adrià's avant-garde methods gained international recognition, and he stands as one of the most important figures in molecular gastronomy.

2. Heston Blumenthal:

Known for his eclectic and experimental approach to cooking, Heston Blumenthal, the chef-owner of The Fat Duck in the UK, has been instrumental in popularizing the concept of molecular gastronomy. Blumenthal's relentless pursuit of understanding the science behind cooking led him to incorporate techniques like sous vide cooking, freeze-drying, and nitrogen freezing in his kitchen. His signature dishes, such as snail porridge and nitro-scrambled eggs, showcased his ability to blend culinary traditions with scientific methods, creating an extraordinary dining experience.

3. Grant Achatz:

Grant Achatz, the head chef of Alinea in Chicago, has been pivotal in elevating molecular gastronomy to new heights. Recognized for his precision, attention to detail, and culinary artistry, Achatz has made an indelible mark on the culinary world. With dishes like edible helium balloons and a suspended dessert created tableside using liquid nitrogen, Achatz showcases his extraordinary skill in transforming ordinary ingredients into extraordinary culinary works of art. Achatz's relentless pursuit of excellence has earned him numerous accolades and cemented his place as one of the most influential chefs in molecular gastronomy.

4. Massimo Bottura:

Massimo Bottura, the renowned chef behind Osteria Francescana in Italy, is known for his inventive and conceptual approach to molecular gastronomy. Bottura's dishes bring together traditional Italian cuisine with avant-garde techniques, resulting in a harmonious amalgamation of flavors, textures, and presentations. Bottura's ability to deconstruct classic Italian dishes and reimagine them in a contemporary context earned his restaurant the title of the world's best restaurant in 2016 and 2018. His creations, such as Oops! I Dropped the Lemon Tart, pushed the boundaries of experimental cooking while paying homage to culinary tradition.

5. José Andrés:

Although not traditionally associated with molecular gastronomy, José Andrés, the Spanish-American chef, has played a significant role in introducing scientific techniques to the culinary world. Andrés combines his passion for molecular gastronomy with his dedication to humanitarian efforts. His non-profit organization, World Central Kitchen utilizes scientific methods and techniques to provide food relief during disasters worldwide. This combination of using scientific principles for social change has given Andrés a unique and influential position in the molecular gastronomy landscape.

These influential chefs have not only transformed culinary trends but have also given birth to a new way of cooking that blends science, artistry, and imagination. With their trailblazing techniques and creativity, they have redefined the possibilities of what cuisine can offer, inspiring a generation of chefs to push boundaries and experiment with their own imaginative culinary creations.

Molecular Gastronomy, a term that has gained popularity in recent years, refers to the scientific study of the physical and chemical processes that occur during cooking. It may sound complicated, but it is actually a fascinating exploration into the world of food, flavors, and textures.

Traditionally, this field of study was limited to the professional chefs in high-end restaurants who sought to push the boundaries of traditional cooking. However, with the rise of social media and cooking shows, the average home cook has become more interested in molecular gastronomy and its applications in their own kitchens.

One of the most intriguing aspects of molecular gastronomy is its ability to transform familiar dishes into stunning works of art. By employing scientific principles and techniques, you can elevate your home-cooked meals to a whole new level. But how does one go about incorporating molecular gastronomy into home cooking?

First and foremost, it is crucial to have a basic understanding of the science behind molecular gastronomy. Some key concepts to get acquainted with include spherification, emulsification, gelification, and foams. Spherification, for example, involves transforming liquids into spheres using additives like sodium alginate and calcium chloride. This technique can be used to create caviar-like balls of various flavors that explode in your mouth.

Once you grasp the fundamental principles, it's time to experiment with ingredients and tools that are commonly used in molecular gastronomy. Some essential items to consider acquiring include a siphon for whipping up flavored foams, a precision scale for accurate measurements, and food-grade chemicals like agar-agar and xanthan gum. These tools and ingredients are the building blocks for creating unique and exciting dishes.

The art of molecular gastronomy lies not only in the final product but also in the presentation. With the help of modern plating techniques, home cooks can transform their dishes into visually stunning masterpieces. From the meticulous arrangement of ingredients to the use of decorative garnishes and sauces, every detail contributes to the overall sensory experience of a dish.

While molecular gastronomy may seem like it belongs only to the realm of professional chefs, it is entirely possible to replicate many of its techniques in a home kitchen. With proper research, experimentation, and a willingness to embrace the scientific side of cooking, you can elevate your home cooking to new heights. Just imagine serving your friends and family a dessert that resembles a piece of art or surprising them with a cocktail that photogenically smokes and changes flavors before their eyes.

As with any new skill or technique, practice makes perfect. Understand that not every experiment will be successful, and some dishes may require several attempts to master. However, the journey of discovering and unlocking the mysteries of molecular gastronomy in your own kitchen is an exciting and worthwhile endeavor.

So, if you're ready to take your culinary skills to the next level, why not dive into the world of molecular gastronomy? With its blend of science and art, this intriguing discipline offers a whole new perspective on home cooking. Tap into your creativity, experiment fearlessly, and you may just become the molecular gastronomist of your household.

Chapter 8: The Zero-Waste Movement in Kitchens

THE ZERO-WASTE MOVEMENT has gained significant momentum in recent years, with more and more individuals and businesses embracing the idea of reducing waste and minimizing their environmental impact. This movement has extended its influence to the kitchen, where initiatives to reduce waste have sprouted, aiming to create sustainable practices that promote efficient resource utilization and minimize landfill contributions. In this chapter, we will delve into the fascinating world of the zero-waste movement in kitchens, exploring its key principles, benefits, and practical tips to make your kitchen a more sustainable space.

1. Key Principles of the Zero-Waste Movement:

The zero-waste movement in kitchens is built upon a few fundamental principles that guide its followers towards sustainable practices:

a. Refusing: One of the core principles of zero-waste is refusing single-use items or products with excessive packaging. Choosing reusable alternatives or refusing altogether helps to reduce unnecessary waste.

b. Reducing: The concept of minimalist consumption is central to the zero-waste movement. By consciously reducing the number of items we own or purchase, we can minimize our waste generation.

c. Reusing: Embracing reusable items fosters resourcefulness and promotes longevity. Reusing containers, shopping bags, and utensils eases our reliance on disposable alternatives, thus reducing waste.

d. Recycling: Although recycling is not the ultimate solution, it plays a significant role in managing waste. Proper recycling practices and creating awareness about recyclable materials can contribute to minimizing landfill waste.

2. Benefits of Embracing Zero-Waste Kitchens:

There are numerous benefits associated with adopting zero-waste practices in the kitchen.

a. Environmental conservation: By curbing waste generation, we help protect the environment by reducing energy consumption, conserving natural resources, and mitigating air and water pollution.

b. Cost savings: Investing in reusable alternatives and reducing wasteful purchases can save a substantial amount of money in the long run. This translates into significant financial benefits for individuals and families.

c. Health improvements: A zero-waste lifestyle encourages the consumption of fresh, whole foods and discourages the use of processed and packaged products that may contain harmful chemicals or additives.

d. Community engagement: Participating in the zero-waste movement creates a sense of community engagement, by connecting individuals with like-minded people who are working towards a common goal of waste reduction and sustainability.

3. Tips for Creating a Zero-Waste Kitchen:

Now that we understand the principles and benefits of the zero-waste movement in kitchens, let's explore some practical tips to help you transform your kitchen into an eco-friendly space:

a. Bulk shopping: Opt for shopping in bulk to minimize excessive packaging. Bring your own reusable containers and buy items such as grains, spices, and snacks from bulk bins to avoid unnecessary waste.

b. Composting: Implement a composting system in your kitchen to divert organic waste from landfills. Composting not only reduces overall waste but produces nutrient-rich compost for your garden.

c. Meal planning and smart shopping: Plan your meals in advance to avoid food waste. Making a shopping list and sticking to it significantly reduces impulse purchases and unnecessary food spoilage.

d. Cutting down on disposables: Swap out disposable paper towels, plastic wrap, and other single-use items for reusable alternatives such as cloth towels, beeswax wrap, and silicone food storage bags. This simple switch can greatly reduce your waste footprint.

e. Repurposing and upcycling: Get creative with repurposing items that would otherwise end up as waste. Old jars can be transformed into storage containers, while vegetable scraps can become flavorful stocks or used for composting.

THE ZERO-WASTE MOVEMENT in kitchens has emerged as a transformative force, encouraging individuals to make conscious choices towards a more sustainable lifestyle. By adhering to the key principles, embracing reusable alternatives, and adopting practical tips, your kitchen can become an eco-friendly space that minimizes waste and contributes to a healthier planet. Join the zero-waste movement in the kitchen today and play your part in creating a more sustainable future.

The zero-waste philosophy is a fairly new concept that is gaining popularity as people become more conscious of their environmental impact. It is centered around the idea of reducing waste to as close to zero as possible in order to minimize the negative repercussions it has on the planet.

To fully understand the zero-waste philosophy, it's important to delve into its principles and the practices that go along with it. Here are some key aspects to consider:

1. Refusing: The first principle of zero waste is refusing what you don't need. This entails refusing single-use items like plastic bottles, bags, and straws. By consciously choosing not to accept these wasteful products, you are taking a significant step towards reducing waste.

2. Reducing: The second principle involves reducing your consumption and overall waste generation. This can be achieved through mindful shopping, buying only what you need, and opting for durable or reusable products instead of disposable ones. By actively reducing your consumption, you minimize your contribution to landfill waste.

3. Reusing: The third principle of zero waste is centered around reusing items whenever possible. This can be done through strategies like repairing broken items instead of immediately replacing them and finding creative ways to repurpose things that would otherwise become waste.

4. Recycling: Recycling is an important solution for waste that cannot be refused, reduced, or reused. However, it is crucial to understand that recycling should be the last resort option in the zero-waste hierarchy. It's essential to

prioritize the first three principles before relying on recycling, as the process itself consumes resources and energy.

5. Composting: Composting forms an integral part of the zero-waste philosophy. By composting organic waste such as food scraps and yard clippings, you can divert them from landfills and create nutrient-rich soil for gardening or farming.

6. Extended Producer Responsibility (EPR): One key concept of zero waste is advocating for EPR, where manufacturers take responsibility for their products' full lifecycle, including the packaging and disposal. Encouraging companies to create recyclable or reusable packaging and designing products with longevity in mind can greatly contribute to reducing waste.

Understanding these principles is essential, but implementing them into daily life requires effort and commitment. Embracing a zero-waste lifestyle involves making conscious choices and investing time and effort to find sustainable alternatives to traditional practices.

In conclusion, the zero-waste philosophy is based on the principles of refusing, reducing, reusing, recycling, composting, and advocating for extended producer responsibility. By embracing these principles, individuals can significantly reduce their waste generation and contribute to a healthier and more sustainable planet.

Zero-waste cooking is a concept that focuses on reducing, reusing, and recycling everything that comes out of our kitchen. It means creating as little waste as possible throughout the cooking process, from buying groceries to transforming leftovers into new meals. Adopting a zero-waste approach not only helps the environment by reducing the amount of trash produced but also saves money by making the most out of your ingredients. Here are some practical tips for zero-waste cooking that you can incorporate into your daily cooking routine.

1. Plan your meals: Before heading to the grocery store, plan your meals for the week ahead. This will help you buy only what you need, reducing the chance of ingredients going to waste. Take inventory of what you already have in your pantry and fridge, and build your meal plan around those items.

2. Shop smart: When shopping for groceries, choose fresh produce that is loose rather than packaged if available. Bring your own shopping bags, produce bags, and containers to avoid using plastic bags provided by the store. Buying in

bulk is another great way to reduce packaging waste. Look for stores that offer bulk bins where you can buy grains, nuts, and spices without extra packaging.

3. Use your scraps: Many vegetable and fruit scraps are edible and can be used in creative ways to reduce waste. Stems, peels, and leaves from vegetables like carrots, beets, and radishes can be used in stews or blended into soups for added flavor. Fruit peels can be used to infuse water or make homemade fruit vinegars. Be creative and find ways to incorporate these usually discarded parts into your cooking.

4. Preserve and store properly: Proper storage plays a crucial role in preventing food waste. Invest in proper storage containers, glass jars, and reusable wraps to keep your ingredients fresh for longer. If you have leftovers, store them in airtight containers and make sure to use them up before they spoil.

5. Embrace wilted or overripe produce: Don't discard produce just because it has started to wilt or become overripe. Instead, find ways to incorporate them into your cooking. Overripe bananas can be mashed and used in baking as a natural sweetener, while wilted greens can be refreshed by soaking them in icy water for a few minutes.

6. Get creative with leftovers: Leftovers are a goldmine for zero-waste cooking. A roasted chicken can be transformed into a hearty soup, leftover veggies can be used to make a frittata or stir-fry, and cooked grains can be turned into a salad or used as a base for grain bowls. Get creative with leftovers and let nothing go to waste.

7. Make your own broth: Vegetable scraps, such as onion peels, carrot tops, and celery leaves, can be collected in a freezer bag and used to make homemade vegetable broth. Similarly, meat bones can be boiled down to make flavorful broth or stock. By making your own broth, you avoid buying pre-packaged ones and ensure that every last bit of flavor is extracted from your ingredients.

8. Compost: Despite your best efforts, there will always be some food waste that cannot be used. Instead of throwing it away, consider setting up a compost system in your kitchen or garden. Composting allows organic waste to decompose and turn into nutrient-rich soil that can be used for gardening or potted plants.

In conclusion, zero-waste cooking is all about being mindful of our food choices and making the most out of every ingredient. By adopting these practical tips, we can reduce waste in the kitchen, save money, and contribute to a more sustainable lifestyle. Happy cooking!

Zero-waste restaurants and chefs are paving the way towards a more sustainable and environmentally-friendly future in the food industry. These culinary pioneers have taken on the challenge of minimizing food wastes in their operations by implementing creative strategies and innovative techniques that not only reduce their ecological footprint but also elevate the dining experience.

One crucial element in achieving zero waste is proper sourcing and selection of ingredients. Chefs committed to this concept prioritize working with local farmers and producers who practice sustainable agriculture and minimize packaging waste. They often establish direct relationships with these suppliers, enabling them to have a better understanding of the entire food chain and reducing the use of intermediaries that contribute to waste.

Moreover, zero-waste restaurants and chefs diligently work on using every part of the ingredient to maximize its potential and minimize waste. This includes utilizing stems, peels, and other typically discarded parts creatively in dishes, thus championing the concept of nose-to-tail or root-to-stem cooking. By promoting a holistic approach to ingredients, these chefs not only reduce waste but also introduce unique flavors and textures into their culinary creations.

In addition to smart ingredient utilization, zero-waste chefs embrace preservation techniques such as pickling, fermenting, and curing to extend the shelf life of food items. By harnessing these traditional methods, they can transform surplus produce into flavorful components that can be used in future dishes, thereby reducing the need to dispose of excess food. This approach also adds an element of depth and complexity to the menu, providing diners with an unforgettable gastronomic experience.

Creative waste management systems are also integral to the success of zero-waste restaurants. Chefs in this arena will often implement composting programs and collaborate with local farmers or community gardens to ensure food scraps are repurposed. Some establishments even source non-edible food waste, such as coffee grounds or grains, to produce biogas and biofertilizers, thereby closing the food waste loop and minimizing their environmental impact.

Zero-waste practices extend beyond the kitchen and into the dining experience itself. These establishments often use reusable, recyclable, or compostable material in their packaging, tableware, and other single-use items. By opting for these environmentally-friendly alternatives, they reduce the amount of waste going to landfills and contribute to a circular economy model.

By putting the principles of zero-waste at the forefront of their operations, these restaurants and chefs become patrons of sustainability and leaders in the fight against climate change. Not only do they have a positive impact on the environment, but they also shape the culinary landscape, inspiring others in the industry to adopt more sustainable practices.

In conclusion, zero-waste restaurants and chefs are revolutionizing the food industry by championing ecologically-conscious practices. Their dedication to minimizing food waste through intelligent ingredient selection, creative utilization, preservation techniques, and innovative waste management systems sets an example for a more sustainable future. These culinary pioneers prove that it is possible to deliver extraordinary dining experiences while concurrently caring for the planet.

In today's fast-paced world, where technology is rapidly advancing and new challenges are constantly emerging, it is essential to stay ahead of the curve. The challenges that enterprises and individuals face in the 21st century are diverse and complex, requiring innovative solutions and a forward-thinking mindset. This article will delve into some of these challenges, as well as provide insights into the future directions that organizations need to consider.

One of the key challenges that organizations face is cybersecurity. With the increasing reliance on digital infrastructure and the rise of threats such as data breaches and hacking, ensuring the safety of sensitive information has become a top priority. Cybersecurity measures need to be constantly updated and strengthened to keep up with the ever-evolving techniques used by hackers.

Another significant challenge is the need to adapt and embrace digital transformation. As technology continues to reshape industries, businesses must be willing to adopt new tools and processes to remain competitive. This often requires a cultural shift within organizations, with leaders needing to encourage innovation and empower employees to explore new ideas.

Furthermore, globalization and the interconnectedness of economies present both opportunities and challenges. On one hand, businesses now have access to a global customer base, allowing for expansion into new markets. On the other hand, competition has intensified, requiring organizations to have a deep understanding of international markets and adapt their strategies accordingly.

Sustainability is another pressing challenge that needs to be addressed. With concerns over climate change and dwindling natural resources, businesses are under increasing pressure to reduce their environmental footprint and adopt sustainable practices. This includes transitioning to renewable energy sources, minimizing waste, and ensuring supply chains adhere to ethical standards.

Additionally, the rapid pace of innovation and technological advancements has brought about disruptions in various industries. Organizations must be prepared to adapt to these disruptions and navigate the uncertainty that comes with them. This often involves a combination of embracing emerging technologies, re-skilling the workforce, and staying agile in the face of constant change.

Looking to the future, there are several key directions that organizations need to consider. Firstly, artificial intelligence and automation will continue to transform various industries. From self-driving cars to AI-powered customer service, businesses need to explore how these technologies can enhance their operations and improve efficiency.

Another important future direction is the increasing importance of data and analytics. As organizations collect vast amounts of data, the ability to effectively analyze and gain insights from this information will become a critical differentiator. Businesses that can harness the power of data to make informed decisions will have a strategic advantage.

Additionally, addressing the growing demand for diversity and inclusivity will be crucial. Organizations need to foster a culture of inclusivity and diversity to attract and retain top talent, as well as better serve a diverse customer base. This requires a commitment to creating equal opportunities and promoting a sense of belonging within the workforce.

Lastly, sustainable practices will become even more important in the future. With increasing concern over climate change and consumer demand for eco-friendly products, businesses need to prioritize sustainability in their operations and supply chains. This includes investing in renewable energy, implementing circular economy principles, and reducing waste across the entire value chain.

In conclusion, the challenges that organizations face in today's dynamic world are diverse and constantly evolving. From cybersecurity to sustainability, businesses must be proactive in addressing these challenges and embracing new technologies and strategies. Looking to the future, organizations need to consider the impact of artificial intelligence, data analytics, diversity, and sustainability on their operations. By staying ahead of the curve, organizations can navigate these challenges and set themselves up for success.

Chapter 9: The Impact of Climate Change on Food

Climate change is one of the defining challenges of our time, and its consequences are far-reaching. From rising temperatures and changing rainfall patterns to more frequent extreme weather events, the impacts of climate change are already being observed in various sectors. One particularly critical area affected by climate change is food production. In this chapter, we delve into the intricate relationship between climate change and food, exploring the ways in which our changing climate poses significant threats to global food security.

Section 1: Changing Growing Conditions

Climate change alters the fundamental conditions required for agriculture, making it increasingly difficult to produce food in certain regions. Throughout history, farmers have adapted and cultivated crops based on predictable climate patterns. However, as these patterns are disrupted, farmers face numerous challenges.

1.1 Rising Temperatures: Global warming leads to higher temperatures, which can cause significant changes in crop growth and development. Heat stress negatively impacts yields for many major staple crops, such as wheat, maize, and rice.

1.2 Alterations in Precipitation: Alterations in rainfall patterns, including shifts in timing, intensity, and distribution, further exacerbate difficulties for farmers. Droughts, floods, and unpredictable precipitation can devastate crops and affect water availability for irrigation.

Section 2: Pests and Diseases

Climate change also has indirect consequences on food production by altering the distribution and behavior of pests and diseases. These changes create new challenges for farmers in their efforts to protect their crops and livestock from such threats.

2.1 Expanding Geographic Range: Warmer temperatures can extend the geographic range of pests and diseases, causing increased occurrences in areas previously unaffected. This expansion can lead to crop losses due to new invasive species or the resurgence of existing pests.

2.2 Altered Lifecycles and Proliferation: Climate change affects the lifecycles of pests and diseases, influencing their reproduction rates and overall abundance. This potential upsurge in the population contributes to increased crop damage and the need for more significant pest management efforts.

Section 3: Altered Ecosystems and Biodiversity

Climate change not only impacts agricultural productivity but also disrupts the delicate balance of ecosystems that support food production.

3.1 Loss of Pollinators: Rising temperatures, habitat destruction, and altered flowering times can lead to declines in pollinator populations. With fewer pollinators, plants struggle to reproduce, resulting in reduced yields for many fruits, vegetables, and nuts.

3.2 Disrupted Fisheries and Aquaculture: The warming of oceans and changes in water chemistry pose significant threats to marine ecosystems, affecting fish populations and marine food webs. This disruption ultimately impacts the availability and access to seafood, a vital protein source for millions worldwide.

Section 4: Implications for Food Security and Nutrition

The combined effects of climate change on agriculture result in numerous implications for global food security and nutrition.

4.1 Decreased Food Availability and Increased Food Prices: Lower agricultural yields and disruptions in supply chains can cause food shortages and price volatility, particularly impacts vulnerable populations.

4.2 Nutritional Deficiencies: Climate change impacts the nutritional content of crops, lowering essential micronutrient concentrations such as iron and zinc. Consequently, malnutrition becomes more prevalent, affecting both developing and developed countries.

4.3 Increased Risks of Foodborne Illness: Changes in temperature and precipitation patterns create favorable conditions for certain foodborne pathogens. This increases the risks of foodborne diseases, posing health risks for consumers.

CHAPTER 9 HAS HIGHLIGHTED the multifaceted impact of climate change on food, emphasizing the pressing need for action. Adapting agricultural practices, investing in resilient infrastructure, and curbing greenhouse gas emissions are crucial steps to mitigate these challenges. While addressing climate change's threat to food security requires a global effort, local action by governments, farmers, and individuals is equally essential for a sustainable future where all can access nutritious and affordable food.

Climate change is a phenomenon that has been happening for decades and is now gaining more attention and concern. It refers to the long-term changes in temperature, precipitation, wind patterns, and other aspects of the Earth's climate system. These changes are primarily caused by human activities, such as the burning of fossil fuels and deforestation, which increase the concentration of greenhouse gases in the atmosphere.

One of the most significant impacts of climate change is the shift in agricultural patterns. Agriculture is one of the most important sectors affected by climate change, as it relies heavily on specific climatic conditions, such as temperature and rainfall, for successful crop production.

Rising temperatures and changing rainfall patterns have profound effects on agricultural productivity. Higher temperatures can lead to increased evaporation, moisture stress, and heat stress on plants. This can result in reduced crop yields and lower quality produce. On the other hand, altering rainfall patterns can lead to droughts and floods, both of which pose significant challenges to farmers.

One of the major consequences of climate change is the alteration of the suitable growing areas for different crops. As temperature and rainfall patterns shift, the regions that were once ideal for specific crops may become less favorable. For example, certain areas that were traditionally suitable for growing wheat may become too warm or receive inadequate rainfall, making it difficult to sustain wheat production. This forces farmers to adapt by either changing the crop they grow or moving to regions with more favorable conditions. Such shifts in agricultural areas can have significant socio-economic implications, as they can disrupt local economies and lead to the displacement of farmers.

Climate change also poses a threat to livestock production. Rising temperatures can increase heat stress on animals, leading to reduced fertility, decreased milk production, and even death in extreme cases. Changing precipitation patterns can also affect the availability and quality of grazing lands, which poses challenges for animal husbandry.

In addition to these direct impacts on agriculture, climate change can also result in an increase in pests and diseases. Warmer temperatures can allow pests and diseases to thrive, causing damage to crops and livestock. This requires farmers to invest more resources in pest control and disease management, which adds additional costs and risks to agricultural production.

To mitigate the negative impacts of climate change on agriculture, various strategies need to be adopted. Improving water management practices, such as rainwater harvesting and efficient irrigation systems, can help farmers cope with changing rainfall patterns. Diversifying crop varieties and adopting new farming techniques, such as conservation agriculture, can also increase the resilience of agriculture to climate change. Furthermore, developing climate-resilient infrastructure and promoting sustainable farming practices can contribute to reducing greenhouse gas emissions and mitigating the effects of climate change.

In conclusion, climate change is disrupting agricultural patterns around the world. Rising temperatures, changing rainfall patterns, and increased incidence of pests and diseases pose significant challenges to crop and livestock production. It is crucial to implement adaptation and mitigation strategies to ensure the sustainability of agriculture in the face of climate change. By taking these measures, we can mitigate the negative impacts on farmers, protect food security, and build a more resilient agricultural sector.

In recent years, the effect of climate change on various aspects of our lives has become increasingly evident. One area that is particularly vulnerable is food production. As temperatures rise, extreme weather events become more frequent, and the availability of water becomes scarce, our ability to produce food is profoundly threatened. However, humans are adaptable creatures, and there are steps that can be taken to mitigate the impact of climate change on food production.

One major challenge in adapting food production to climate change is water scarcity. As rainfall patterns shift and become less predictable, irrigation systems that depend on steady water supplies are rendered less effective. To address this, farmers need to implement water-saving techniques such as drip irrigation and precision watering. These methods ensure that water is used more efficiently, reducing waste and conserving this valuable resource. Additionally, investing in advanced technologies such as soil moisture sensors and weather forecasting can help farmers make more informed decisions about irrigation schedules and effectively manage water usage.

Another critical aspect of food production affected by climate change is soil quality. Higher temperatures and increased frequency of extreme weather events can degrade soil, leading to erosion and reduced fertility. One approach to combat this is implementing sustainable farming practices. Rotating crops, cover cropping, and reduced tillage can enhance soil health and structure, improving its resilience to climate-induced challenges. Moreover, incorporating organic matter into the soil through composting and carbon sequestration techniques can help mitigate the adverse effects of climate change on soil quality.

Furthermore, adjusting cropping patterns can contribute to adapting food production to a changing climate. As certain regions become more prone to droughts, floods, or heatwaves, farmers need to diversify their crop choices. Planting a variety of crops that are more resilient to different climate conditions ensures a more secure yield in the face of unpredictable weather. Additionally, growing crops with shorter growing cycles can help mitigate the risks associated with extremes in weather patterns.

The entwined relationship between agriculture and climate makes the task of adapting food production all the more crucial for our future. Thankfully, technological advancements in plant breeding offer promising solutions to enable crops to cope with growing climate challenges. By identifying and utilizing crop varieties with traits that can withstand heat stress, water scarcity, or other climate-induced conditions, farmers can boost their resilience against climate change.

Another avenue to adapt food production to climate change is promoting agroforestry and diversifying agricultural landscapes. Planting trees and shrubs alongside crops provides shade and windbreaks, mitigating some of the impacts of high temperatures and strong winds. Moreover, agroforestry systems increase biodiversity, which can help maintain the health of ecosystems and promote natural pollination and pest control.

Lastly, it is crucial to invest in research and development to find innovative approaches to adapting food production to climate change. Through collaborations between scientists, farmers, and policymakers, we can develop new technologies, breeding methods, and farming practices that are specifically tailored to address the challenges posed by climate change. Governments and organizations should provide incentives and financial support to encourage the adoption of sustainable and climate-smart agriculture.

In conclusion, adapting food production to climate change is a complex and multifaceted task. It requires a combination of sustainable farming practices, water conservation techniques, adjusted cropping patterns, technological advancements, and promoting agroforestry. By implementing these measures and investing in research and development, we can build a resilient and sustainable food system capable of withstanding the challenges of a changing climate. The future of food production depends on our ability to adapt and innovate, ensuring food security for generations to come.

Climate change is a pressing issue that affects every aspect of our lives, including agriculture. As precipitation patterns shift, temperatures rise, and extreme weather events become more common, farmers face incredible challenges in maintaining their food production. However, there is hope in the form of climate-resilient crops and techniques that can help mitigate these challenges.

One of the key components of climate-resilient agriculture is the cultivation of climate-resilient crops. These are plant varieties that have been bred to tolerate the stresses associated with climate change. For instance, heat-tolerant varieties of crops such as maize, rice, and wheat have been developed to withstand higher temperatures. These crop varieties have been selected through meticulous breeding techniques that involve identifying and crossing plants with desirable traits such as drought resistance, disease resistance, and efficient water usage.

Another important aspect of climate-resilient agriculture is the adoption of new techniques and practices that can better withstand climate change impacts. Conservation agriculture is one such technique that advocates for minimal soil disturbance, permanent soil cover, and diversified crop rotations. This helps protect soil structure and health, reduces erosion, and improves water retention capacity. By implementing conservation agriculture, farmers can better adapt to changing climatic conditions and ensure their agricultural systems remain sustainable.

In addition to conservation agriculture, water management techniques play a crucial role in climate-resilient farming. With changing rainfall patterns, efficient water usage becomes even more important. Techniques like drip irrigation, micro-sprinklers, and rainwater harvesting support effective water management on farms, ensuring that crops receive adequate water while using it efficiently.

Another innovative approach in climate-resilient agriculture is agroforestry. Agroforestry involves the integration of trees and shrubs with crops and livestock systems. By providing shade, windbreaks, and additional sources of income through timber and fruits, agroforestry systems enhance the resilience of farming systems. Additionally, trees act as carbon sinks, helping to mitigate climate change by sequestering carbon dioxide from the atmosphere.

Furthermore, integrating livestock into farming systems can also contribute to climate resilience. Mixed farming, where crops and animals are managed together, creates synergies that increase the overall productivity and profitability of the farm. Moreover, well-managed animal husbandry practices that prioritize animal welfare and efficient resource utilization reduce greenhouse gas emissions.

Promoting biodiversity is another crucial component of climate-resilient agriculture. Diverse cropping systems that incorporate a wide range of species and varieties increase ecosystem resiliency and reduce the risk of crop failure due to climate-related stresses. Additionally, the preservation and restoration of natural habitats and landscapes can enhance biodiversity and ecological services such as pollination and pest control.

To achieve widespread adoption of climate-resilient crops and techniques, farmers need access to technical knowledge, quality seeds, and appropriate financial resources. Effective extension services, farmer-to-farmer learning networks, and public-private partnerships can play instrumental roles in promoting and disseminating climate-resilient practices. Moreover, supportive policies and incentives that prioritize sustainable farming systems can encourage the adoption of climate-resilient agriculture at a global scale.

In conclusion, climate-resilient crops and techniques provide hope for farmers facing the challenges of climate change. By cultivating crop varieties that can withstand shifting climatic conditions, adopting conservation agriculture practices, implementing efficient water management techniques, integrating agroforestry and livestock, promoting biodiversity, and ensuring access to necessary resources and knowledge, farmers can build resilience and sustain their agriculture systems in the face of a changing climate.

In addressing the challenges posed by climate change on our food system, it is crucial to recognize the multi-faceted role of both policy and consumers. Policy plays a significant role in shaping the trajectory of our food system, setting the guidelines and strategies to ensure its resilience and sustainability in a changing climate. At the same time, consumer behavior and choices play a crucial role in driving demand, influencing the type and sourcing of food, and ultimately shaping the overall food system.

Effective policy measures are essential for creating an enabling environment that incentivizes climate-adaptive food production and consumption. Governments should prioritize investing in research and development to foster the innovation of climate-resilient agricultural practices and technologies. This can include the development of drought-resistant crop varieties, precision farming techniques, and sustainable irrigation systems. Furthermore, policies should promote sustainable land management practices, conservation of biodiversity, and the protection of natural resources, such as water and soil.

Policy frameworks should also ensure that farmers have access to finance, insurance schemes, and technical support to implement climate-adaptive practices. Financial incentives, such as subsidies or tax breaks, can encourage farmers to adopt climate-smart agriculture techniques, which not only reduces their vulnerability to climate change but also improves the overall resilience of the food system. In addition, policies should be designed to support small-scale farmers, who are most vulnerable to the impacts of climate change, and ensure their inclusion in the decision-making and policy formulation process.

Beyond policy, consumer behavior plays a critical role in shaping the demand for climate-adaptive food. Increasing consumer awareness and education about the impacts of climate change on the food system is essential. People need to understand how their food choices can contribute to either exacerbating or mitigating climate change. Sustainable and climate-friendly food choices should be promoted at all levels, from educational institutions to public campaigns and labeling systems.

Consumers can play an active role in reducing their carbon footprint and supporting climate-adaptive food systems by choosing locally sourced, seasonal produce. Food that is grown closer to home requires fewer resources for transportation and storage, reducing greenhouse gas emissions. Moreover, reducing meat consumption or transitioning to plant-based diets can have a substantial positive impact on greenhouse gas emissions, as the livestock sector is a major contributor to global emissions.

In addition, supporting farmers who embrace climate-adaptive practices through purchasing decisions is crucial. Consumers can look for certifications and labels such as Organic, Fair Trade, or Rainforest Alliance, as these often signify sustainable and climate-friendly practices. By choosing products from companies that prioritize climate resilience, consumers demonstrate the demand for such practices and contribute to building a market for climate-adaptive food.

Furthermore, consumers can participate in local food initiatives, such as community-supported agriculture (CSA) programs or farmers' markets. These initiatives connect consumers with local farmers, ensure traceability, and promote sustainable and climate-adaptive food production systems. By actively engaging in such initiatives, consumers not only support local economies but also foster resilience in food systems by reducing the dependence on long and vulnerable supply chains.

To conclude, policy and consumer role are both crucial in building climate-adaptive food systems. Policy measures that incentivize sustainable and climate-smart agricultural practices, protect natural resources, and support small-scale farmers are essential. Simultaneously, consumer choices in favor of sustainably sourced, locally produced, and plant-based foods contribute to shaping resilient food systems. The partnership between policy and consumers is integral to creating a climate-resilient and sustainable food future.

Chapter 10: Health Trends and Dietary Shifts

I n the last few decades, there has been a significant shift in the way people perceive health and wellness. As society becomes more aware of the impact of diet on overall well-being, health trends and dietary shifts have gained momentum. This chapter will delve into the various health trends that have emerged and explore the underlying reasons for these dietary shifts.

1. Organic and Eco-Friendly Foods:

One prominent health trend that has captured the attention of consumers worldwide is the preference for organic and eco-friendly foods. Concerns about pesticide residues, genetically modified organisms (GMOs), and the impact of conventional farming practices on the environment have led to a surge in demand for organic produce. Increasingly, consumers are choosing products that are free from harmful chemicals and supportive of sustainable farming practices.

2. Plant-Based Diets:

The rise of plant-based diets, specifically vegetarian and vegan lifestyles, has been a substantial dietary shift observed in recent years. With growing concerns about animal welfare, environmental sustainability, and health benefits, many individuals are opting to exclude or significantly reduce their consumption of animal products. Plant-based diets emphasize the consumption of fruits, vegetables, legumes, and whole grains, which are abundant in essential nutrients and have been linked to decreased risks of chronic diseases.

3. Awareness of Food Allergies and Intolerances:

In the past, food allergies and intolerances often went undiagnosed or were erroneously labeled as vague digestive issues. However, the rise in awareness and testing methodologies has resulted in an increased understanding of these conditions. Individuals are now more knowledgeable about their specific food allergies and intolerances, leading to substantial changes in their dietary choices. Free-from food ranges, gluten-free products, and allergen labeling have become increasingly prevalent to accommodate these dietary shifts.

4. Functional Foods and Nutraceuticals:

Functional foods and nutraceuticals are another health trend contributing to dietary shifts. As consumers become more proactive about their health, they are seeking out foods and beverages with added health benefits. From fortified cereals to probiotic yogurts and antioxidant-rich superfoods, functional foods provide additional nutrients or bioactive compounds that promote specific health outcomes. The demand for these products has skyrocketed as consumers increasingly view food as a means to improve their well-being.

5. Paleo and Keto Diets:

The Paleo and Keto diets have gained immense popularity due to their promoted weight loss benefits and perceived overall health improvements. The Paleo diet advocates for consuming foods that our ancestors would have eaten during the Paleolithic era, primarily focusing on meat, fish, fruits, vegetables, and nuts while excluding grains, legumes, and dairy. Likewise, the Keto diet centers around low-carbohydrate, high-fat foods, which are believed to facilitate weight loss and improve energy levels. These dietary shifts have garnered attention for their potential benefits, although their long-term effects on health remain a subject of ongoing debate.

THE SHIFTING DIETARY trends observed in recent years reflect the growing emphasis placed on health, sustainability, and individualized nutrition. This chapter explored various health trends, such as the rise of organic and eco-friendly foods, plant-based diets, awareness of food allergies and intolerances, functional foods and nutraceuticals, and the popularity of Paleo and Keto diets. As consumers continue to prioritize wellness and seek out dietary choices that align with their values, it will be interesting to witness further innovations and shifts in the food industry to meet these evolving demands.

In recent years, there has been a growing awareness about the impact of food choices on our health and well-being. As a result, there has been a shift in global diets towards more nutritious and balanced meals. In this article, we will explore some of the current health trends in global diets and their impact on our overall health.

Plant-Based and Vegan Diets:

One of the most significant dietary trends in recent years is the surge in popularity of plant-based and vegan diets. Many people are now opting to reduce their consumption of animal products and instead focus on plant-based alternatives. This shift is driven by various factors, including ethical concerns about animal welfare, environmental sustainability, and the potential health benefits.

Plant-based diets involve consuming predominantly plant-derived foods, such as fruits, vegetables, whole grains, legumes, nuts, and seeds, while limiting or excluding animal-derived products. Vegan diets, on the other hand, completely eliminate all animal products, including meat, dairy, eggs, and honey.

These types of diets have been linked to various health benefits, including a reduced risk of chronic diseases such as heart disease, obesity, and Type 2 diabetes. Plant-based and vegan diets tend to be high in fiber, vitamins, and minerals, while being low in saturated fats and cholesterol, making them a popular choice for those looking to improve their health.

Sustainable and Local Sourcing:

Rising concerns about the environmental impact of food production have also led to an increased emphasis on sustainable and local sourcing of food. Consumers are becoming more conscious of the carbon footprint associated with importing food from distant regions and recognize the benefits of supporting local farmers and markets.

Sustainable diets aim to minimize the negative impact of food production on the planet by promoting sustainable farming practices, reducing waste, and prioritizing seasonal and local produce. By consuming foods that are grown closer to home, greenhouse gas emissions from transportation can be significantly reduced. Additionally, purchasing from local sources promotes community health and helps to strengthen local economies.

Healthy Snacking:

Snacking is a common eating habit, but people are now looking for healthier alternatives to traditional processed snacks. In order to meet this demand, a wide range of nutritious snacks, such as vegetable chips, granola bars, and fruit and nut mixes, has emerged in the market.

These healthier snack options provide consumers with the convenience and pleasure of snacking while offering nutrient-rich ingredients. By choosing healthier snacks, individuals can fuel their bodies with wholesome nutrients rather than empty calories from sugary or processed options. This trend encourages mindful snacking and contributes to a more balanced and nutritious diet overall.

Functional Foods and Supplements:

As people become increasingly interested in optimizing their health, there has been a surge in the consumption of functional foods and supplements. Functional foods are those that offer additional health benefits beyond their basic nutritional value. They often contain bioactive compounds, such as antioxidants, omega-3 fatty acids, or probiotics, which can improve specific aspects of health.

Examples of functional foods include fortified cereals, yogurts with added probiotics, and beverages enriched with vitamins and minerals. Additionally, dietary supplements, such as vitamins, minerals, and herbal extracts, are gaining popularity among individuals seeking targeted health benefits.

While functional foods and supplements can be beneficial for certain individuals with specific needs or deficiencies, it is important to note that a well-balanced diet should always be the primary source of nutrients. Consulting with healthcare professionals is crucial to ensure that these products are used appropriately and safely.

In conclusion, current health trends in global diets revolve around adopting plant-based and vegan diets, emphasizing sustainable and local sourcing, choosing healthier snacks, and incorporating functional foods and supplements. These trends reflect a growing understanding of the profound impact that food choices have on our health, as well as the desire to create a healthier and more sustainable future. Embracing these trends can have long-lasting benefits, helping individuals make positive changes to their diet and overall well-being.

10.2 Nutritional Science and Public Health

Nutritional science plays a crucial role in public health by examining the effects of food and nutrition on human health and disease. With the rise in chronic diseases, such as heart disease, obesity, and diabetes, the field of nutritional science has become more important than ever in guiding public health policies and interventions.

One of the primary goals of nutritional science is to understand the biological processes by which nutrients are metabolized and utilized by the body. This knowledge helps in determining the optimal intake of various nutrients and designing dietary guidelines that promote health. Researchers study the effects of different macro and micronutrients, such as carbohydrates, proteins, fats, vitamins, and minerals, on various aspects of health, including metabolism, immune function, and disease prevention. This information forms the basis for developing evidence-based dietary guidelines that cater to populations with specific nutritional needs.

Public health initiatives, supported by nutritional science, focus on preventing and managing nutrition-related diseases. For example, the promotion of healthy eating behaviors and the prevention of childhood obesity are major public health concerns. Nutritional scientists conduct research to understand the factors contributing to obesity, such as excessive calorie intake and sedentary lifestyles. They work collaboratively with public health officials to develop programs that educate and encourage healthy eating habits, physical activity, and the availability of nutritious foods in schools, workplaces, and communities.

Additionally, nutritional science and public health collaborate in advocating policy changes to improve population health outcomes. This includes regulations on food labeling, advertising, and availability. Nutritional scientists research the impact of food marketing techniques on consumer choices and behavior. With this information, public health organizations can make evidence-based policy recommendations to promote healthier food environments.

Another important area where nutritional science intersects with public health is in the field of food insecurity and malnutrition. Globally, millions of people suffer from inadequate access to nutritious food, resulting in nutrient deficiencies and poor health outcomes. Nutritional scientists and public health professionals collaborate to identify vulnerable populations and develop strategies to address food insecurity through programs such as food assistance, community gardens, and nutrition education.

Moreover, nutritional science research plays an important role in identifying the relationship between nutrition and the prevention or management of chronic diseases. Obesity, cardiovascular disease, cancer, and diabetes are highly prevalent conditions influenced by dietary choices. Researchers study the effects of different diets and specific nutrients on these diseases. Armed with this knowledge, public health policies can promote interventions ranging from dietary guidelines for disease prevention to nutrition therapy recommendations for disease management.

In conclusion, nutritional science and public health are interconnected and play vital roles in promoting population health. Through research, policy development, and community interventions, nutritional science provides vital information to public health professionals, laying the foundation for effective strategies to combat chronic diseases, promote healthy eating habits, address food insecurity, and improve overall health outcomes for all.

Diet plays a significant role in maintaining good health. It provides essential nutrients that support physiological functions and helps prevent the development of chronic diseases. Over time, diet patterns have shifted dramatically in many parts of the world due to factors such as industrialization, urbanization, globalization, and changes in food production and consumption practices. These diet shifts have had profound implications on individuals' health, with a significant increase in the prevalence of chronic diseases.

The shift towards a more Westernized diet, characterized by a high intake of refined grains, processed foods, added sugars, and unhealthy fats, has been linked to the rising burden of chronic diseases. This diet is typically low in fruits, vegetables, whole grains, and lean proteins. These dietary changes have contributed to an increase in obesity rates, and a higher risk of developing conditions such as type 2 diabetes, cardiovascular diseases, certain types of cancer, and metabolic syndrome.

One of the main driving factors behind these dietary shifts is the convenience factor. In today's fast-paced world, processed and ready-to-eat meals have become the norm. These food options are often high in calories, added sugars, unhealthy fats, and sodium. They are also low in essential nutrients, such as fiber, vitamins, and minerals. The ease of access to these foods, coupled with aggressive marketing and advertising campaigns, has influenced individuals' food choices, leading to a decreased consumption of nutrient-dense foods.

One major consequence of these dietary shifts is the growing epidemic of obesity and its associated health complications. Obesity has become a major risk factor for chronic diseases. The excessive calorie intake, coupled with a sedentary lifestyle, disrupts the body's energy balance, leading to weight gain. The excess body weight places additional stress on various body systems, increasing the risk of developing conditions such as hypertension, dyslipidemia, and insulin resistance.

Moreover, the high intake of added sugars, particularly in the form of sugary beverages, has been strongly linked to obesity and chronic diseases. For instance, the regular consumption of sugary drinks has been associated with an increased risk of developing type 2 diabetes, cardiovascular diseases, and metabolic syndrome. These beverages provide empty calories and contribute to excessive weight gain, as they do not provide any essential nutrients.

Another important aspect of the diet shift is the decreased consumption of whole grains, fruits, and vegetables. These foods are rich in dietary fiber, vitamins, minerals, antioxidants, and phytochemicals that are vital for overall health. The abandonment of traditional dietary patterns that emphasize these components in favor of refined grains and processed foods has resulted in a decreased intake of essential nutrients, which can predispose individuals to chronic diseases.

Fortunately, there has been a growing awareness of the impact of diet on chronic diseases, leading to a resurgence of interest in healthier eating habits. As a result, there has been a shift towards conscious dietary choices such as increased consumption of whole foods, organic produce, and plant-based diets. These dietary patterns have been associated with numerous health benefits, including a reduced risk of chronic diseases.

In conclusion, diet shifts characterized by a higher intake of processed and unhealthy foods have contributed to the rising burden of chronic diseases globally. These dietary changes, including a decrease in the consumption of nutrient-dense foods and an increase in added sugars and unhealthy fats, have resulted in increased rates of obesity, type 2 diabetes, cardiovascular diseases, certain types of cancer, and metabolic syndrome. However, there is now an increasing understanding of the importance of healthier dietary choices and a trend towards more wholesome and plant-based foods. With continued efforts to promote and educate individuals about the benefits of a balanced diet, it is hoped that the burden of chronic diseases will be reduced, leading to better overall health and well-being.

In the realm of health and nutrition, countless advancements have been made over the past few decades. From groundbreaking research in medicine to the rising awareness around the power of a balanced diet, the field has witnessed remarkable progress. However, these achievements merely set the stage for even more exciting developments in the future. The anticipated future outlook on health and nutrition is both promising and enlightening.

One significant trend set to shape the future of health and nutrition is personalization. With advancements in technology, particularly in artificial intelligence and genomics, health professionals will have access to more refined and accurate data about individuals. This will enable them to create personalized treatment plans and nutrition recommendations based on an individual's genetic makeup, lifestyle, and other relevant factors. Personalization will not only enhance the effectiveness of treatments but also revolutionize preventive healthcare.

Another direction that the future holds is the integration of traditional and complementary medicine into mainstream healthcare. Traditional medicine systems such as Ayurveda, Traditional Chinese Medicine, and herbal therapy have long been used to promote health and wellness in various cultures. Increasing scientific validation and cultural acceptance now position these ancient practices as reliable alternatives or complements to conventional medicine. As a result, future health and nutrition strategies will likely incorporate the best of both worlds, offering patients a comprehensive approach to their well-being.

Advances in technology will continue to play a vital role in shaping the future outlook for health and nutrition. Wearable devices and health monitoring apps are already changing the way individuals manage their wellness. In the near future, these technologies will likely become even more sophisticated, giving individuals real-time information about their vital signs, nutrition intake, and physical activities. This heightened level of self-awareness will empower individuals to make more informed decisions about their health while promoting preventive measures.

Furthermore, the emerging field of nutrigenomics holds incredible promise for personalized nutrition. Nutrigenomics explores the interaction between an individual's genes and their food choices. By understanding how different nutrients interact with specific genes, researchers can develop personalized dietary recommendations tailored to an individual's genetic makeup. This exciting field has great potential to prevent and manage chronic diseases like diabetes, obesity, and cardiovascular conditions more effectively.

In addition to personalized approaches, sustainable nutrition is expected to garner more attention in the future. As the world grapples with significant issues such as climate change, food insecurity, and environmental degradation, the need for sustainable dietary practices becomes crucial. The future of health and nutrition will likely emphasize plant-based diets, incorporating more fruits, vegetables, nuts, and grains into people's daily routines. This shift not only improves human health but also mitigates the environmental impact of animal agriculture and reduces greenhouse gas emissions.

It is important to acknowledge that with these advancements, accessibility to health and nutrition services must be prioritized to avoid exacerbating existing health inequities. Ensuring that all individuals have access to personalized treatments, alternative therapies, and technological innovations should be an essential focus in the coming years. Additionally, educating the population about the potential benefits of personalized medicine, sustainable nutrition, and complementary medicine will be crucial to foster widespread acceptance and understanding.

In conclusion, the future outlook on health and nutrition paints an exciting picture of personalized, integrative, and sustainable approaches. Advancements in technology, particularly in artificial intelligence and genomics, will allow for unprecedented personalization of healthcare plans. The integration of traditional and complementary medicine will provide individuals with a comprehensive approach to well-being. Furthermore, the emergence of nutrigenomics and sustainable nutrition practices will enable targeted dietary recommendations and a reduced environmental footprint. It is imperative that future developments prioritize accessibility and education to ensure an inclusive and informed society. The potential for transformative changes in health and nutrition is limitless, and the future promises a healthier and sustainable world for all.

Chapter 11: The Rise of Food Apps and Online Delivery

In recent years, the technological revolution has transformed almost every aspect of our daily lives, and the food industry is no exception. The rise of food apps and online delivery has revolutionized the way we order and consume food. Through these platforms, consumers can explore a plethora of culinary options, order their favorite dishes with a few taps on their smartphones, and have them delivered right to their doorstep. In this chapter, we will delve into the fascinating world of food apps and online delivery, uncovering the reasons behind their rapid rise and the profound impact they have had on the food industry.

The Birth of Food Apps:

The first food apps emerged in the early 2010s, capitalizing on the increasing dependence on smartphones and the growing shift towards digital platforms for convenience. These apps offered an entirely new way for consumers to explore local restaurant menus, read reviews, and place orders, all from the convenience of their own devices. The likes of Grubhub, Uber Eats, and Postmates quickly gained popularity, paving the way for further innovation in the industry.

Benefits of Food Apps and Online Delivery:

One of the primary reasons for the exponential growth in food apps and online delivery is the unparalleled convenience they offer. No longer are consumers bound by the constraints of opening hours or the need to physically go to a restaurant. With a few taps, a wide variety of culinary delights can be delivered directly to their desired location, at any time of the day. This convenient option has not only proven highly popular among busy professionals but has also opened new avenues for catering to people with limited mobility or accessibility.

Furthermore, food apps provide consumers with extensive menus and the ability to browse and compare different restaurants, ensuring they can find the perfect meal to suit their preferences. Online reviews and ratings also boost transparency, giving users insights into the quality and experience offered by various establishments, enabling them to make informed decisions.

The Impact on the Food Industry:

The rise of food apps and online delivery has had a transformative effect on the traditional food industry. Restaurants that were once exclusively brick-and-mortar establishments now find themselves embracing online platforms to cater to the growing demand for digital ordering. This shift has presented both opportunities and challenges, as restaurants strive to optimize operations to handle the influx of online orders, while also capitalizing on the increased visibility that online platforms provide.

The increased demand for online delivery has also resulted in the emergence of ghost kitchens and virtual restaurants. These entities operate solely for delivery purposes, without a physical dining area, allowing entrepreneurs to experiment with new culinary concepts and reduce overhead costs. This innovative and cost-effective model has opened up a whole new realm of possibilities for culinary entrepreneurs.

Challenges and Future Outlook:

While the rise of food apps and online delivery has revolutionized the food industry, it has not been without its challenges. Many small, independent restaurants struggle to keep up with the high commission fees charged by these platforms, cutting into their traditionally slim profit margins. Additionally, the escalation of delivery services has put additional strain on the already stretched gig economy workforce, raising questions about fair pay and worker rights.

Looking to the future, the rise of food apps and online delivery shows no signs of slowing down. The convenience and accessibility they offer continue to captivate consumers, while technological advancements such as drone deliveries and Artificial Intelligence-powered order recommendations promise to push the boundaries even further. As the industry evolves, it will be important to strike a balance between profitably supporting small businesses and ethical treatment of workers within the food delivery ecosystem.

THE RISE OF FOOD APPS and online delivery has ushered in a new era of convenience and accessibility for consumers, transforming the way we order and consume food. These platforms have not only empowered consumers with an extensive array of culinary options but have also altered the landscape of the food industry itself. Restaurants have adapted to meet the demand for online delivery, while entrepreneurs have seized the opportunity to explore new culinary concepts. Despite the challenges that come with this technological revolution, the future looks promising as further innovation continues to reshape the way we experience food.

The evolution of online food services has been a fascinating journey, showcasing the ever-growing capabilities of technology and the changing needs and preferences of consumers. From humble beginnings to the sophisticated platforms we see today, online food services have transformed the way people order, receive, and enjoy their meals.

In the early days of online food services, ordering food online was a novelty. It started with basic websites where customers could select items from a limited menu and have it delivered to their doorstep. These early services laid the groundwork for what was to come, setting the stage for a rapidly evolving industry.

One significant development in the evolution of online food services was the introduction of mobile apps. With the widespread adoption of smartphones, apps became the go-to method of ordering food online. Companies like Uber Eats, DoorDash, and GrubHub took advantage of this shift, creating user-friendly interfaces that allowed customers to browse menus, place orders, and track deliveries, all from the convenience of their phones.

As the demand for online food services skyrocketed, newer platforms emerged, offering a wider range of options. Meal-kit delivery services like Blue Apron and HelloFresh gained popularity, providing customers with pre-portioned ingredients and recipes that they could prepare at home. This allowed people to enjoy restaurant-quality meals in the comfort of their own kitchens, eliminating the need to dine out or order takeout.

Another significant evolution in online food services was the rise of third-party delivery services. Initially, restaurants would handle their own deliveries, but as the demand increased, these services stepped in to bridge the gap. Companies like Seamless and Postmates formed partnerships with various restaurants, offering their delivery infrastructure to ensure customers received their food promptly.

Furthermore, technology played a crucial role in enhancing the efficiency and customization of online food services. Artificial intelligence and machine learning algorithms were employed to predict customer preferences and offer personalized recommendations. These algorithms studied past orders, customer reviews, and even dietary restrictions to suggest dishes that aligned with individual preferences.

The COVID-19 pandemic further accelerated the growth of online food services, as social distancing guidelines and lockdown measures limited in-person dining and increased the reliance on food delivery. Many restaurants embraced these services for the first time, adapting their business models to survive the unprecedented challenges.

Looking ahead, the future of online food services appears promising. We can expect further advancements in delivery technology, such as the use of drones and autonomous vehicles, to improve speed and efficiency. Additionally, the integration of virtual assistants and voice recognition technology could simplify the process of ordering food, making it even more effortless for consumers.

In conclusion, the evolution of online food services has come a long way, revolutionizing the way people order and enjoy their meals. From basic websites to sophisticated apps and personalized recommendations, these services have adapted to meet the changing needs of consumers. With technology continuously advancing, we can only anticipate further innovation in this thriving industry.

11.2 Food Apps: Convenience and Challenges

Food apps have become increasingly popular in recent years, offering users the convenience of ordering food with just a few taps on their smartphones. These apps have revolutionized the way we dine, making it easier than ever to get our favorite meals delivered straight to our doorstep. However, amidst all the convenience, there are also several challenges that come with using food apps.

One of the main benefits of food apps is the convenience they offer. With these apps, you no longer have to spend time calling restaurants to place an order or waiting in long queues at your favorite eateries. Instead, you can simply browse through the menu options in the app, select your desired items, and proceed to checkout. This streamlined process saves time and effort, particularly for individuals with busy schedules or limited access to nearby restaurants.

Another convenience of food apps is the ability to customize your order according to your preferences. Many apps provide options for selecting ingredients, toppings, and even portion sizes, allowing users to tailor their meals to their specific tastes and dietary needs. This added flexibility makes it easier for individuals with dietary restrictions or allergies to find suitable options and ensures that everyone can enjoy their desired meal without any complications.

Additionally, food apps often offer a wide range of cuisine options, providing users with numerous choices and the opportunity to explore different food cultures. From traditional favorites to international delicacies, these apps open up a world of culinary possibilities, making it easier than ever to satisfy your cravings and try something new.

However, despite the many conveniences that food apps bring, there are also several challenges associated with their use. One major challenge is the potential lack of quality control. When ordering through an app, you do not have the ability to personally assess the food's quality or freshness. This can result in unfortunate experiences where the delivered meal does not meet your expectations, leading to disappointment and dissatisfaction.

Furthermore, food apps are often accompanied by additional fees and delivery charges. While the convenience they offer justifies some of these expenses, excessive fees might make the dine-in option more economically viable for some individuals. Additionally, certain restaurants may choose not to partner with food apps, limiting the range of options available. This can make it challenging for users to find their preferred dining establishments on these platforms.

Finally, reliance on food apps can lead to a decrease in social interaction and a decrease in the experiential aspect of dining out. Going to a restaurant offers the opportunity to socialize, enjoy ambiance, and experience the flavors and aromas in person. By ordering through apps, these aspects are diminished, and the dining experience becomes more about convenience than enjoying the complete culinary experience.

In conclusion, food apps have brought undeniable convenience to the world of dining. They offer personalized customization, a wide range of cuisine options, and save time and effort. However, challenges such as potential quality control issues, additional expenses, and a decrease in experiential dining must be considered. Despite the challenges, food apps remain a popular choice for many, offering convenience and opening doors to a variety of culinary experiences.

Local food businesses have been significantly impacted by the ongoing coronavirus pandemic that has swept across the globe. From restaurants and cafes to small food shops and markets, these businesses have seen a tremendous decline in revenue and face an uncertain future.

One of the primary challenges for local food businesses has been the implementation of lockdown measures and social distancing protocols. Many restaurants and cafes were forced to close their doors temporarily, relying on takeout and delivery services as their only means of continued operation. The sudden shift to a predominantly digital platform required adapting to new technologies and investing in online infrastructure, which proved to be an extra burden for already struggling businesses.

Furthermore, the closure of non-essential shops and restrictions on daily movement have drastically reduced foot traffic in local food markets. These markets, often known for their vibrant and diverse offerings, have seen a significant decline in customers. Small traders who rely on local markets for their livelihoods have been hit hard, struggling to make ends meet and facing unique challenges in selling perishable products.

Moreover, supply chain disruptions caused by border closures and logistical challenges have caused many local food businesses to face shortages of essential ingredients and products. Import restrictions and trade disruptions have created obstacles for sourcing ingredients from abroad, forcing businesses to heavily rely on local suppliers. This has resulted in increased costs and limited options for menu or product offerings.

Despite these challenges, some local food businesses have found ways to adapt and even thrive during these difficult times. Many restaurants and cafes have turned to offering meal kits or DIY cooking experiences, allowing customers to recreate their favorite dishes in the safety of their own homes.

Some have even collaborated with other local businesses to offer mixed food and beverage boxes, pooling resources and generating cross-promotion.

There is also growing support for local food businesses, as more consumers recognize the importance of sustaining these establishments during this crisis. Customers are actively seeking out ways to support their favorite local cafes, restaurants, and shops. The rise of online platforms and social media has provided an avenue for businesses to engage directly with their customers, sharing updates on operations, menu changes, and community initiatives.

However, it's important to acknowledge that the road to recovery for local food businesses will likely be long and challenging. It will require continued support and collective action from consumers, policymakers, and communities. Initiatives such as financial aid programs, rent relief, and promotional campaigns can play a crucial role in helping these businesses rebound.

In conclusion, the impact of the coronavirus pandemic on local food businesses has been substantial. From closures and changing operating models to supply chain disruptions, these businesses have faced numerous challenges. However, with the support of their communities and adaptive strategies, many local food businesses have shown resilience and the potential for recovery. As we navigate through this crisis, it is important to recognize and value the role that these businesses play in our communities and work towards creating a sustainable future for them.

With the increasing reliance on technology and changes in consumer behavior, the online food ordering and delivery industry has witnessed tremendous growth in recent years. However, the future of this industry holds even greater promise, as technological advancements and shifting trends continue to shape its landscape.

One of the key trends that will dominate the future of online food ordering and delivery is the advent of artificial intelligence (AI) and machine learning. As AI continues to evolve, it will play a crucial role in improving the efficiency and effectiveness of the overall delivery process. By analyzing past data, AI algorithms can accurately predict order patterns, optimize delivery routes, and reduce delivery times. This will result in enhanced customer satisfaction and increased profitability for businesses operating in this sector.

Furthermore, AI-powered chatbots will become an integral part of online food ordering platforms. Chatbots will be able to assist customers in placing orders, providing personalized recommendations, and addressing queries or concerns. This enhanced customer service experience will not only attract more users to these platforms but will also streamline the ordering process, contributing to increased user retention.

Additionally, the future of online food ordering and delivery will witness a significant focus on personalization. Companies will utilize customer data and AI algorithms to create personalized menus, recommendations, and promotions based on each user's preferences. By tailoring their offerings to individual taste profiles, online food ordering platforms will be able to provide a unique and customized experience to each customer, enhancing their overall satisfaction and loyalty.

Moreover, there will be a growing emphasis on sustainability within the industry. Consumers are becoming increasingly conscious of their environmental impact and are demanding eco-friendly food delivery options. In response to this demand, online food ordering and delivery platforms will invest in environmentally friendly practices such as using electric or hybrid delivery vehicles, implementing packaging solutions with minimal waste, and promoting the use of local and organic ingredients. This green shift will not only cater to the evolving consumer preferences but will also differentiate businesses in a competitive market.

Another significant aspect of the future of online food ordering and delivery is the integration of emerging technologies such as virtual reality (VR) and augmented reality (AR). VR and AR can offer an immersive and interactive experience for customers who can virtually browse through menus, visualize food items, and even see how their dish is being prepared in real-time. This transformative technology will revolutionize the way consumers interact with digital menus and make food choices, further enhancing the convenience and excitement of online food ordering and delivery.

Lastly, the future of online food ordering and delivery will witness a shift towards multi-channel platforms. Presently, customers primarily place orders through dedicated mobile applications or websites. However, in the future, it is likely that online food delivery will be seamlessly integrated into various platforms such as social media platforms, messaging apps, and smart home devices. This integration will enable customers to place orders through their preferred channels, thereby increasing accessibility and convenience.

In conclusion, the future of online food ordering and delivery holds immense potential. With advancements in AI, personalized experiences, sustainable practices, integration of emerging technologies, and multi-channel platforms, the industry is set to revolutionize the way people order and receive food. As consumers continue to seek convenience, customization, and efficiency, the online food ordering and delivery sector will adapt and innovate to meet their evolving needs.

Chapter 12: Indigenous Foods and Traditional Practices

Indigenous foods and traditional practices play a crucial role in the cultural heritage and well-being of indigenous communities worldwide. This chapter aims to provide a comprehensive overview of the diverse range of indigenous foods and traditional practices, ranging from agricultural techniques to culinary traditions.

Section 1: Agricultural Techniques

1.1 Shifting Cultivation:

Shifting cultivation, also known as slash-and-burn agriculture, is a traditional agricultural practice employed by many indigenous communities. This technique involves clearing small plots of land, burning the vegetation, and cultivating crops for a few years until the soil fertility declines. Subsequently, the plot is left to regenerate, and the community moves on to a new area. Shifting cultivation allows indigenous people to maintain sustainable farming methods while preserving the balance of their surrounding ecosystems.

1.2 Terracing:

Terracing is another ingenious agricultural technique utilized by indigenous communities in mountainous regions. It involves cutting sloping hillsides into a series of steps, creating flat fields for planting crops. Terraces facilitate effective water management, preventing erosion and helping improve soil quality. Additionally, the stepped formation utilizes gravity to distribute water evenly throughout the fields, ensuring optimal growth for crops.

1.3 Intercropping and Companion Planting:

Indigenous farmers also employ methods like intercropping and companion planting to maximize productivity and nutrient cycling. Intercropping involves planting different crops within the same field simultaneously. By doing so, indigenous communities can benefit from higher yields and reduced pest infestations. Companion planting focuses on the intentional pairing of plants that provide mutual benefits, such as repelling pests, enriching soil nitrogen, or enhancing pollination.

Section 2: Culinary Traditions

2.1 Wild Harvesting:

One hallmark of indigenous culinary traditions is the utilization of wild-harvested foods. Indigenous communities have developed an intimate understanding of their surrounding environments, allowing them to identify and gather an array of edible plants, mushrooms, seafood, and game meat. These wild-harvested foods not only offer unique flavors and textures but are often nutritionally dense, showcasing the ingenuity and resourcefulness of indigenous cuisines.

2.2 Traditional Food Preservation:

Preserving food effectively is crucial for communities lacking access to modern techniques. Indigenous communities have perfected traditional methods of food preservation such as smoking, drying, fermenting, and pickling. These processes not only increase the longevity and availability of locally sourced ingredients but also enhance their flavors. Examples include the production of pemmican, a concentrated dried meat mixed with fat and berries, and fermentation of vegetables to produce sauerkraut or kimchi.

2.3 Food Rituals and Customs:

Food holds significant cultural and spiritual value for indigenous communities, often taking center stage in various rituals and customs. These practices reinforce the connection between people, nature, and the spiritual world. Ceremonial feasts and gatherings help maintain social cohesion and preserve cultural practices and identity within indigenous communities.

INDIGENOUS FOODS AND traditional practices serve as valuable repositories of knowledge and culture, reflecting the deep connection between indigenous communities and their environments. Through sustainable agricultural techniques, culinary traditions, and food-related customs, indigenous peoples continue to nurture their cultural heritage and promote biodiversity preservation. Recognizing the importance of indigenous foods and traditional practices is vital for sustaining the well-being of indigenous communities while fostering respect and understanding of their cultural contributions to the world.

One cannot fully understand the complexities of Indigenous food systems without embarking on a deep exploration of its origins, intricacies, and importance within Indigenous cultures. Indigenous food systems are unique and diverse, reflecting the deep-rooted connection between Indigenous peoples and their land.

The foundations of Indigenous food systems can be traced back thousands of years, deeply intertwined with the traditional knowledge and sustainable practices developed by Indigenous communities. These systems are characterized by their holistic approach, viewing food as much more than mere sustenance. Indigenous peoples recognize the interconnectedness of all living beings and understand that the food they consume is deeply linked to their spiritual, physical, and cultural well-being.

From hunting, gathering, and fishing to sophisticated agricultural practices, Indigenous food systems represent a profound understanding of the natural world. Traditional Indigenous knowledge includes the cultivation and preservation of a wide variety of crops, as well as the careful management of wild food resources such as fish, game, and medicinal plants. Such knowledge has been passed down through generations, adapting to the local environment and allowing for the continued survival and thriving of Indigenous communities.

Indigenous food systems are also intimately connected to the concept of food sovereignty. Food sovereignty refers to the right of communities to define their own systems of food production and distribution in ways that are culturally, socially, and environmentally appropriate. In order to achieve food sovereignty, Indigenous peoples are reclaiming control over their traditional lands, waters, and resources, ensuring that decisions about food production are made by the community members themselves.

Exploring Indigenous food systems is not only a journey into cultural heritage and environmental stewardship but also a platform for expressing resilience and reclaiming Indigenous identity. These systems provide a basis for community cohesion and empowerment, offering opportunities for sustainable economic development, and strengthening ties with ancestral traditions.

In recent times, there has been a growing recognition of the importance of Indigenous food systems beyond Indigenous communities themselves. The wider world is beginning to recognize the value of Indigenous knowledge in terms of sustainable agriculture, biodiversity conservation, climate change adaptation, and the preservation of traditional livelihoods.

However, it is essential to acknowledge that these systems face numerous challenges and are under constant threat. Colonization, industrialization, and the modern agricultural system have often marginalized, disrupted, and disrespected Indigenous food systems. Land degradation, the loss of biodiversity, and the introduction of non-traditional crops and agricultural practices have had damaging repercussions on Indigenous communities' ability to maintain their food sovereignty.

To address these challenges, it is necessary to engage in a collaborative approach, respecting and learning from Indigenous wisdom and practices. Governments, non-governmental organizations, and the wider society play crucial roles in supporting Indigenous food systems and ensuring their sustainability.

Exploring Indigenous food systems can be a transformative experience, offering insights into the intricate relationship between people, nature, and food. It sparks discussions on the need for a more inclusive, regenerative, and sustainable approach towards food production and consumption. By embracing the diversity and resilience inherent in Indigenous food systems, we can cultivate a better future for all.

Preservation of traditional food practices is a crucial aspect of cultural heritage and is essential for the continuity of cultural identity and the understanding of our ancestral traditions. Such practices are deeply rooted in history and reflect the beliefs, lifestyles, and values of communities across the globe. However, in recent years, the advent of modernization has brought forth significant changes in our food habits, leading to the gradual erosion of traditional food practices.

Traditional food practices are often intricately linked to local ecosystems and are developed to suit specific geographical and climatic conditions. They are passed down through generations orally, thereby building a strong communal bond and creating a sense of shared history. These food practices encompass not only the cultivation of specific crops but also the ways of harvesting, cooking, and consuming meals. These practices vary from region to region, reflecting the diversity in cultural practices, dietary preferences, and religious beliefs.

Additionally, traditional food practices are constructed to ensure sustainable farming methods that encourage the conservation of biodiversity and the protection of fragile ecosystems. For instance, certain indigenous farming techniques integrate traditional knowledge in soil conservation, water management, and forest preservation. These methods promote soil fertility, minimize land degradation, and reduce carbon emissions, contributing to environmental sustainability.

Moreover, traditional food practices often emphasize seasonality, local produce, and a healthy balance of nutrients. These practices encourage the consumption of diverse foods and the avoidance of processed and industrialized products. As the world witnesses an alarming rise in chronic diseases associated with the overconsumption of unhealthy processed food, traditional food practices provide an important lesson in promoting a sustainable and balanced diet.

Despite the numerous benefits associated with traditional food practices, several challenges threaten their preservation. The fast-paced lifestyle and the homogenization of food cultures due to globalization have led to a decline in traditional culinary practices. Furthermore, the corporatization of food production, promotion of monoculture agriculture, and the rise of mass-produced products have marginalized traditional farmers and undermined local food systems.

In order to preserve traditional food practices, various steps can be taken. Firstly, there should be concerted efforts to document and pass on traditional knowledge and practices to future generations. This can be done through oral histories, written records, and digital platforms. Collaboration between older generations and young researchers can help in the documentation process and ensure the continuity of traditional practices.

Secondly, initiatives should focus on imparting education and awareness about the importance of traditional food practices and their benefits. By teaching young people about their cultural heritage, the significance of these practices can be instilled in the next generation, encouraging them to carry forward the tradition themselves.

Furthermore, governments and organizations should support small-scale farmers practicing traditional agriculture through financial incentives, capacity-building programs, and access to markets. By providing them with the necessary resources and support, traditional food practices can be sustained and celebrated.

Lastly, promoting community-led movements and cultural festivals that celebrate local cuisine and traditional food practices can create awareness and foster a sense of pride and belonging among the community members. It can also generate income opportunities for local food processor and culinary entrepreneurs, facilitating economic development at the grassroots level.

In conclusion, the preservation of traditional food practices is crucial for maintaining cultural diversity, environmental sustainability, and individual well-being. By preserving and promoting these practices, we not only honor our cultural heritage but also contribute to creating a more resilient and harmonious world. It is our collective responsibility to ensure that future generations have the opportunity to appreciate and embrace the rich tapestry of traditional food practices.

In recent years, there has been a growing trend in modern cuisine to incorporate indigenous knowledge and ingredients. This movement not only showcases the rich culinary traditions of Indigenous communities but also promotes sustainable practices and highlights the importance of local and seasonal produce.

Indigenous knowledge refers to the collective wisdom, practices, and beliefs of Indigenous peoples that have been passed down from generation to generation. This knowledge encompasses a broad range of subjects, including agriculture, medicine, spirituality, and food. Indigenous communities have a deep understanding of their local ecosystems, the environment, and the plants and animals that inhabit it. This knowledge has been shaped and refined over centuries and has proven to be incredibly valuable in promoting biodiversity, sustainability, and respect for the land.

One of the most exciting aspects of incorporating Indigenous knowledge into modern cuisine is the utilization of traditional ingredients. Many Indigenous communities have long relied on a variety of unique and nutrient-rich foods that are often overlooked in mainstream cuisine. These can include wild game, fish, edible insects, various types of seaweed, and a plethora of plants and herbs with incredible medicinal properties.

Chefs and food enthusiasts have started to embrace these ingredients, incorporating them into their menus and creating innovative and flavorful dishes. For example, Pacific Northwest Indigenous cuisine features traditional seafood, such as salmon and mussels, paired with native fruits and vegetables like berries and wild onions. The result is a refreshing and authentic representation of the local Indigenous culture that satisfies both the taste buds and the soul.

Another important aspect of incorporating Indigenous knowledge in modern cuisine is the emphasis on sustainable farming and harvesting practices. Indigenous communities have long practiced a deep respect for the earth and have developed methods that preserve and enhance biodiversity. By incorporating these practices into modern food production, we can help mitigate ecological damage and promote healthier ecosystems for future generations.

Additionally, the integration of Indigenous knowledge into modern cuisine can help preserve cultural traditions that might otherwise be lost. By showcasing the culinary heritage of Indigenous communities, we honor their culture and foster a deeper appreciation and understanding of their contributions to our global food landscape. It is through this merging of ancient wisdom and innovative techniques that we can continue to evolve our culinary traditions and create a more inclusive culinary world.

In conclusion, the incorporation of Indigenous knowledge in modern cuisine is a powerful way to celebrate and respect the diverse cultures and ecosystems of our world. By utilizing traditional ingredients, embracing sustainable practices, and honoring Indigenous traditions, we can create a culinary experience that is not only delicious but also socially and environmentally responsible. Let us continue to explore and embrace this vibrant fusion of culinary traditions and build a future for food that is both flavorful and sustainable.

Ethical considerations and cultural appropriation are two important aspects that should be taken into account in any creative process or expression. This is especially true in the world of art, design, fashion, and other creative industries, where diverse cultures are constantly influencing and inspiring artists.

Cultural appropriation refers to the adoption, borrowing, or utilization of elements from a culture that is not one's own, often without understanding the cultural significance behind these elements. While cultural exchange can be positive and enriching, cultural appropriation becomes problematic when it involves the commodification of a culture or misrepresentation of its traditions, beliefs, or practices. This can contribute to the erasure of marginalized cultures, perpetuate stereotypes, and lead to cultural dilution or misappropriation.

One ethical consideration regarding cultural appropriation is respect for the communities or individuals whose culture is being appropriated. Artists and designers should strive to approach cultural inspiration with sensitivity and without the intention to exploit or profit from it without proper acknowledgment. It is important to engage in thorough research and understanding of the cultural context, history, and significance of the elements being utilized.

Furthermore, consent and collaboration are crucial ethical considerations when working with elements from a specific culture. It is important to seek permission and involve members of that community in the creative process, respecting their expertise and rights when representing their culture. This can help ensure proper cultural interpretation and representation, promoting mutual understanding and appreciation.

Another ethical consideration is the power dynamics involved in cultural appropriation. Often, the cultures being appropriated are those belonging to marginalized groups who have historically faced discrimination and oppression. In such instances, cultural appropriation can perpetuate power imbalances, reinforce stereotypes, and further marginalize these communities. Artists should be mindful of these power dynamics and actively work to dismantle such systems through proper representation, education, and advocacy.

Furthermore, ethical considerations extend beyond just the act of appropriation itself. Artists and designers should consider the impact of their work on the culture being represented, as well as its potential effects on a broader societal level. This entails examining the intentions behind the work, the message being conveyed, and the potential consequences of misrepresentation or dilution of cultural heritage.

It is essential to foster a culture of appreciation, respect, and understanding when it comes to cultural exchange and inspiration. This can be achieved through open dialogue, collaboration, and education that promotes cross-cultural understanding and appreciation. By striving for mutual respect and positive engagement with diverse cultures, artists and designers can avoid unethical practices and contribute to a more inclusive and culturally conscious creative industry.

Chapter 13: Food as Art – Culinary Aesthetics

In recent years, the concept of food as art has gained significant recognition in the culinary world. The idea that the presentation, flavors, and overall experience of a dish can be artistic in nature has intrigued chefs and food enthusiasts alike. In this chapter, we will explore the aesthetics of food, delving into the various elements that make a dish visually appealing, harmonious in taste, and emotionally engaging.

Section 1: The Visual Feast

1.1. Aesthetics in plating: Just as a painter carefully chooses colors and brushstrokes, a chef meticulously arranges every component on the plate. We will delve into the importance of color, symmetry, balance, and the use of negative space in creating visually stunning dishes.

1.2. The role of tableware: The choice of plates, glasses, and utensils can greatly enhance the visual appeal of a dish. We will explore how chefs select the perfect tableware to complement their culinary creations.

Section 2: The Symphony of Flavors

2.1. Flavor combinations: Similar to a composer's skillful arrangement of musical notes, chefs aim to create harmonious flavors by using complementary or contrasting ingredients. We will delve into the principles of flavor pairing and how it contributes to the overall taste experience.

2.2. Textures and mouthfeel: Just as texture creates depth and dimension in a painting, chefs manipulate textures in dishes to provide added sensory pleasure. We will explore the interplay between softness, crispiness, creaminess, and other textural elements.

Section 3: Emotions on the Plate

3.1. Storytelling through food: Like a novel or a movie evokes emotions, food can narrate tales and evoke sentimental memories. We will investigate how chefs incorporate storytelling into their culinary creations, bringing forth nostalgia, happiness, or even a sense of discovery.

3.2. Culinary experiences: Restaurants are increasingly utilizing multi-sensory techniques to enhance the dining experience. From visually stunning presentations to interactive dishes, we will explore how chefs transport diners into immersive gastronomic journeys.

Section 4: Food as Fine Art

4.1. Culinary art exhibitions: In recent years, galleries and museums have exhibited visionary food installations and edible artwork. We will investigate the intersection of food and fine art, exploring how renowned artists blur the line between the two worlds.

4.2. Food photography and social media: The rise of food photography on platforms like Instagram has brought a new dimension to culinary aesthetics. We will discuss how food presentations are carefully crafted for the camera and how social media has shaped culinary aesthetics.

FOOD HAS TRANSCENDED its basic purpose of sustenance and transformed into an ever-evolving art form. From stunning visual presentations and harmonious flavors to emotional storytelling and culinary experiences, food has established itself as a multi-faceted artistic medium. In this chapter, we have explored the fascinating world of culinary aesthetics and the immense creativity that chefs bring to the table.

The intersection of food and art has been a subject of fascination for centuries. Both food and art are ancient forms of human expression, and when brought together, they create a sensory experience like no other. Whether it is through painting, sculpture, photography, or performance, artists have found countless ways to explore and celebrate the beauty and significance of food.

Food has long been a source of inspiration for visual artists. The ancient Egyptians, for example, depicted elaborate feasts in their tomb paintings, showcasing the abundance and diversity of food available to their society. Similarly, in the European Renaissance, artists such as Giuseppe Arcimboldo created whimsical and fantastical portraits entirely composed of fruits, vegetables, and other edible elements. These artworks not only captured the aesthetic qualities of the food but also symbolically represented ideas such as abundance, fertility, and the cycle of life.

In the realm of sculpture, food has been sculpted into exquisite and intricately detailed pieces of art. The ancient Greeks, renowned for their appreciation of beauty, crafted extraordinary marble sculptures of food and beverages, which were often left as offerings to the gods. From delicate fruit baskets to ornate wine jugs, these sculptures stood as testaments to the significance of food in ancient Greek culture.

As photography emerged as an art form in the 19th century, food soon became a favored subject. Artists such as Edward Weston and Irving Penn pushed the boundaries of food photography, capturing the textures, colors, and shapes of ingredients and dishes in breathtaking detail. Through close-ups and unconventional compositions, they elevated the everyday act of eating into a moment of visual contemplation.

The intersection of food and art has also found expression in performance art. One notable example is the work of American artist Marina Abramović. In her famous piece, The Artist is Present, Abramović sat silently at a table in a museum for three months, inviting visitors to sit across from her and share a moment of connection. The table between them was starkly bare, emphasizing the importance of human presence and interaction. The absence of food in this piece serves as a reminder that the act of sharing a meal transcends the physical nourishment it provides, offering a deeper sense of connection and understanding.

Today, the relationship between food and art continues to evolve and inspire. Social media platforms are filled with photographs of elaborately plated dishes, captivating food installations at festivals, and food-themed collaborations between artists and chefs. Artists continue to push the boundaries of traditional art forms, exploring new mediums and techniques to capture the essence of food.

The intersection of food and art offers a window into our history, culture, and the way we perceive and appreciate the world around us. It celebrates the human need for sustenance and creativity, reminding us of the profound impact and role that food plays in our lives.

In the culinary world, presentation is just as important as taste when it comes to creating a memorable dining experience. Over the years, chefs and food experts have pushed the boundaries of traditional plating techniques to create truly innovative and visually stunning dishes. This article explores some of the most exciting advancements and aesthetic innovations in plating and presentation.

One of the most notable developments in recent years is the use of molecular gastronomy techniques to transform ingredients into unexpected textures and shapes. This trend has led to the emergence of dishes that are not only delicious but also visually captivating. Chefs are now using various scientific processes such as spherification, foam creation, and emulsification to experiment with the physical properties of food, resulting in unique presentations that challenge what we traditionally consider to be a meal.

Another trend that has gained momentum is the use of edible flowers and microgreens as a way to add color and vibrancy to a dish. These natural ingredients not only provide a visual feast for the eyes but also contribute to the overall taste profile of a dish. Chefs are carefully selecting and delicately placing these decorations to create visually appealing and Instagram-worthy plates of food.

Aesthetic innovations have also introduced a new focus on the use of negative space on a plate. This technique involves strategically placing elements of a dish in a way that creates visually striking arrangements while also emphasizing the main ingredient. The skilled use of empty space allows the diner to appreciate the delicate composition of each individual component and adds a sense of artistry to the overall presentation.

Inspired by the minimalistic approach of Japanese cuisine, chefs have started to incorporate traditional Japanese plating techniques, such as the use of pristine white ceramics and the concept of negative void to create captivating compositions. These techniques focus on simplicity and balance, with an emphasis on clean lines and the meticulous arrangement of ingredients. Such aesthetics not only enhance the visual appeal of a dish but also evoke a sense of tranquility and harmony.

Technology, too, has played a significant role in aesthetic innovations in plating and presentation. High-tech tools like 3D printers are being used to create intricate and geometric garnishes, adding a new dimension to the dining experience. Chefs can now explore textures and designs that were previously impossible, resulting in stunning and visually striking presentations.

Ultimately, the world of plating and presentation is consistently evolving, with chefs continuously seeking new ways to captivate diners' eyes before they even take the first bite. Through experimental techniques, creative use of natural ingredients, focus on negative space, incorporation of Japanese aesthetics, and integration of technology, chefs are pushing the boundaries of what is possible in the world of culinary art. These aesthetic innovations in plating and presentation not only created more visually stunning dishes but also enhanced the overall dining experience and reinforced the notion that food can truly be a transformative and artistic medium.

Culinary artists are not just chefs who know how to cook delicious dishes. They are individuals who possess a unique philosophy and approach to the culinary arts. These artists view food as more than just sustenance; it is an art form that connects people, evokes emotions, and tells stories.

One key element of a culinary artist's philosophy is creativity. These artists constantly push boundaries and experiment with different flavors, textures, and presentations. They believe that meals should be visually appealing, engaging all the senses, and leaving a lasting impression on the diner. The creativity of culinary artists is not limited to the kitchen; it extends to sourcing ingredients, developing recipes, and even designing the restaurant space itself.

Another important aspect of a culinary artist's philosophy is the emphasis on quality. These artists take pride in using the freshest, highest quality ingredients available. They understand that the quality of ingredients directly impacts the final dish, and they strive to source from local, sustainable farms and suppliers. They believe that each ingredient has its own story and brings its unique flavor profile to the table.

Simplicity is also valued by culinary artists. They understand that sometimes less is more, and by using fewer ingredients, the natural flavors can shine through. Culinary artists often use minimalistic plating techniques, allowing the dish to speak for itself. They create balance and harmony with their use of flavors, ensuring that no one element overpowers the others.

Culinary artists also embody a philosophy of seasonality. They believe in using ingredients that are at their peak, both in flavor and nutritional value. They understand that different seasons bring different ingredients, and they embrace the challenges and opportunities associated with changing menus with the seasons. By honoring seasonality, culinary artists support sustainable practices and contribute to the local food ecosystem.

Beyond the food itself, culinary artists also value the concept of hospitality. They believe that dining should be an experience that goes beyond just eating. They strive to create a welcoming and comfortable atmosphere, making every guest feel like a cherished friend. Culinary artists understand that the ambiance, service, and interactions with the staff are just as important as the food itself in creating a memorable dining experience.

Lastly, culinary artists have a deep appreciation for the cultural and historical significance of food. They understand that food is a powerful medium for expressing culture, heritage, and traditions. They research and explore different cuisines, techniques, and ingredients from around the world, combining them to create unique and flavorful dishes that honor culinary traditions while embracing innovation.

In conclusion, culinary artists are artists with a distinctive philosophy and approach to the culinary arts. They see food as more than just a source of sustenance; it is a form of artistic expression that connects people, evokes emotions, and tells stories. Through their emphasis on creativity, quality, simplicity, seasonality, hospitality, and cultural appreciation, culinary artists transform meals into extraordinary experiences.

13.4 Food Styling and Photography

Food styling and photography is a fascinating aspect of the culinary world that has gained immense popularity in recent years. It is the art of making food look beautiful and appetizing for photographs or videos. This field requires a unique skill set that combines knowledge of cooking techniques, artistic ability, and photography skills.

Food styling involves the careful arrangement and presentation of food in a way that enhances its visual appeal. This can include choosing the right props, such as plates, utensils, and other decorative elements, to complement the dish. It also involves various techniques like garnishing, plating, and lighting to create a visually stunning composition.

The purpose of food styling is to make the viewer feel a strong desire to taste and indulge in the dish. It plays a crucial role in advertising, as it has the power to influence consumer behavior and attract customers to certain food products or restaurants. Well-styled and photographed food entices people through social media platforms, cookbooks, magazines, and advertisements.

Food photography, on the other hand, involves capturing images of the styled food. It requires an understanding of lighting, composition, and camera settings to create enticing visuals. This can be challenging as food can often be difficult to capture due to its various textures, temperatures, and colors.

Professional food photographers often use specific techniques and equipment to capture the perfect shot. This includes the use of natural light or artificial lighting setups, diffusers, reflectors, and lenses that allow for close-up shots to highlight the food's details. Post-production editing is also a common practice to enhance the colors, contrast, and overall appearance of the photograph.

Food styling and photography has become an integral part of the culinary world, not only for marketing purposes but also for sharing recipes and culinary experiences. Nowadays, food blogs and social media platforms are flooded with visually stunning images of food, and the demand for well-executed food styling and photography continues to grow.

For aspiring food stylists and photographers, there are various courses, workshops, and resources available to learn the craft. Understanding the fundamentals of cooking, composition, and photography is essential to excel in this field. It requires a keen eye for detail, creativity, and a passion for the culinary arts.

In conclusion, food styling and photography are exciting fields that combine culinary skills with artistic abilities. This aspect of the culinary world plays a significant role in attracting consumers, promoting food products, and sharing gastronomic experiences. With the increasing demand for visually appealing food content, food styling and photography have become invaluable skills for chefs, culinary professionals, and food enthusiasts alike.

Chapter 14: Nutrition and Technology – Personalized Diets

In recent years, nutrition and technology have become inseparable companions in the quest for healthier diets. Personalized diets, also known as precision diets or tailored nutrition plans, have emerged as a revolutionary approach to individualized nutrition. This chapter delves into the world of nutrition and technology, exploring how personalized diets have the potential to reshape the way we eat and optimize our health.

The Role of Technology in Personalized Diets

Advancements in technology have paved the way for the development of personalized diets. With the rise of smartphones, wearable devices, and cutting-edge health tracking apps, individuals can now track their dietary intake, physical activity levels, and even their biological markers with ease.

These technological developments allow for the collection of vast amounts of data, enabling nutritionists and scientists to gain valuable insights into individual nutrition needs. Personalized diets utilize this data, along with information such as genetic profiles, lifestyle factors, and personal preferences, to create tailored nutrition plans for individuals.

The Potential of Genetic Profiling

One crucial aspect of personalized diets is genetic profiling. By analyzing an individual's genetic makeup, researchers can identify specific genetic variants that play a role in their nutrition needs. These genetic variants may affect how individuals metabolize certain nutrients, their sensitivity to food components, and even their predisposition to certain dietary-related health conditions.

For instance, an individual with a genetic variant that affects their ability to metabolize carbohydrates efficiently may benefit from a lower carbohydrate intake. Genetic profiling helps identify such variations, allowing personalized diets to optimize nutrition intake based on an individual's genetic needs.

The Role of Nutritional Apps and Devices

Nutritional apps and wearable devices have significantly contributed to the popularity of personalized diets. These intuitive apps help individuals monitor their dietary intake by allowing them to log their meals, track macronutrient breakdown, and monitor their calorie intake. By synchronizing with other health tracking devices, these apps provide a comprehensive overview of an individual's physical activity levels, sleep patterns, and even stress levels – all vital factors in personalized diet planning.

Furthermore, certain apps utilize artificial intelligence algorithms to provide real-time feedback on meal choices, suggesting alternatives to meet an individual's nutritional goals and alerting them to potential dietary shortcomings. This real-time guidance and support can prove invaluable in maintaining an individual's adherence to their personalized diet plan.

Challenges and Advances

While the concept of personalized diets offers immense promise, several challenges need to be addressed for its widespread adoption. Firstly, accessing high-quality genetic profiling remains costly. However, with advancements in gene sequencing technologies, costs are decreasing, increasing the accessibility of genetic profiling.

Privacy concerns also surround the integration of technology in personalized diets. Given the sensitive nature of genetic data and personal health information, ensuring secure platforms and strict data protection measures is crucial to maintain user trust.

Despite these challenges, advances in technology continue to reshape the field of personalized diets. The development of personalized nutrition algorithms and machine learning algorithms aim to provide more accurate and reliable insights into personalized nutrition goals. This integration of advanced technology with nutrition science can enable individuals to achieve optimal health outcomes through individualized, tailor-made diets.

Conclusion

In Chapter 14, we have explored the remarkable integration of nutrition and technology in the realm of personalized diets. With the assistance of advanced technology, personalized diets have the potential to revolutionize the way we eat, optimizing our health by tailoring nutrition plans to our unique needs and goals. While challenges remain, the relentless progress in genetic profiling, nutritional apps, and machine learning algorithms promises a future where personalized diets become the norm, improving our overall well-being.

Personalized nutrition refers to the idea of tailoring dietary recommendations and interventions to an individual's unique genetic makeup, lifestyle, and specific health goals. It is based on the understanding that each person has a distinct response to different foods and nutrients, and that a one-size-fits-all approach to nutrition may not be ideal for optimal health outcomes.

Advances in technology, such as genomic testing and precision medicine, have enabled researchers to uncover the complex interplay between genetics, metabolism, and nutrition. By analyzing an individual's genetic profile, scientists can identify specific genes that influence how our bodies process and respond to different nutrients. This knowledge forms the basis for personalized nutrition, as it allows healthcare practitioners and nutritionists to recommend a diet that is specifically tailored to an individual's genetic predispositions.

For example, individuals who carry certain gene variants associated with impaired glucose metabolism may benefit from a low-carbohydrate diet, which can help stabilize and regulate blood sugar levels. On the other hand, individuals with a particular variation in a gene associated with increased fat metabolism may thrive on a higher fat intake.

In addition to genetics, personalized nutrition takes into account other factors, such as an individual's lifestyle, current health status, activity levels, and dietary preferences. It acknowledges that different individuals may have different nutrient requirements and tolerances. For instance, a person who follows a vegetarian or vegan lifestyle would require personalized recommendations to ensure they are meeting their nutrient needs, especially for key nutrients like vitamin B12 or omega-3 fatty acids that are commonly found in animal products.

One of the main benefits of personalized nutrition is its potential to prevent or manage chronic diseases. For instance, personalized dietary interventions can be used to address risk factors associated with conditions like obesity, diabetes, and heart disease. By targeting an individual's unique needs, personalized nutrition goes beyond generic dietary guidelines and can offer more precise and effective strategies to improve health outcomes.

To implement personalized nutrition, several approaches can be used. These include:

1. Genetic testing: Analysis of an individual's genetic profile can help identify specific gene variants associated with nutritional needs and preferences. For instance, genetic tests can provide information about lactose intolerance, caffeine metabolism, or sensitivity to saturated or monounsaturated fats.

2. Nutrient tracking: Regular monitoring of nutrient intake, either through food diaries or smartphone apps, can provide insights into an individual's current dietary habits and nutritional gaps. This data can then be used to tailor recommendations and suggest specific dietary changes.

3. Biomarker analysis: Measuring biomarkers, such as blood sugar levels, cholesterol levels, or inflammation markers, can give a more comprehensive view of an individual's health status and response to different dietary interventions. This objective data can guide the development of personalized nutrition plans.

4. Technology-based solutions: Advances in digital health technology, such as wearable devices, can provide real-time feedback on an individual's activity levels, sleep patterns, and dietary habits, assisting in the personalized monitoring and optimization of nutrition.

However, it is important to note that personalized nutrition is still an emerging field, and more research is needed to validate its effectiveness and explore its potential limitations. The interpretation of genetic data and its translation into meaningful dietary recommendations can be complex, and ethical considerations of genetic testing and data privacy need to be a priority.

In conclusion, the concept of personalized nutrition holds promise in providing tailored dietary interventions for individuals based on their genetic makeup, lifestyle, and health goals. By considering factors such as genetics, lifestyle, and dietary preferences, personalized nutrition aims to optimize health outcomes and prevent or manage chronic diseases. Further research and advancements in technology will be critical in unlocking the full potential of personalized nutrition.

The use of technology in assessing nutritional needs has revolutionized the way healthcare professionals approach and address this critical aspect of patient care. No longer confined to manual calculations and guesswork, technology has provided us with accurate and efficient tools to evaluate and monitor individuals' nutritional requirements.

One such technology is the use of mobile applications that help track and analyze dietary intake. These apps allow individuals to record their daily food and beverage consumption, enabling them to gain insights into their nutritional habits. The app calculates the macronutrient and micronutrient content of their diet, providing them with valuable information about their nutrient intake. Health professionals can also use these apps to monitor their patients' nutrition and make any necessary adjustments.

Another groundbreaking technology is the development of wearable devices that track body metrics, such as heart rate, sleep patterns, and physical activity. These devices can also provide users with information on energy expenditure. By combining this data with dietary information gathered through mobile applications, individuals and healthcare professionals can gain a comprehensive understanding of an individual's nutritional status.

Additionally, a more recent advancement in technology is the use of body scanners and imaging techniques to assess body composition. This involves the use of machines that measure parameters such as body fat percentage, muscle mass, and bone density. Not only does this aid in identifying individuals at risk of inadequate nutrition or obesity, but it also helps in developing personalized nutritional plans and monitoring progress over time.

Genetic testing is yet another technological tool that is gaining popularity in assessing nutritional needs. By analyzing an individual's genetic profile, healthcare professionals can identify specific genetic variants related to metabolism and nutrient absorption. This information can help tailor personalized dietary recommendations based on an individual's genetic predisposition, addressing any genetic factors that could impact their nutritional requirements.

Moreover, through the use of electronic medical records (EMRs) and health informatics, healthcare professionals can efficiently analyze and interpret large amounts of data related to nutrition. EMRs allow for accurate documentation of nutritional information, such as detailed dietary histories and specific nutrient requirements for patients with chronic conditions. Data mining and data analysis techniques support healthcare professionals in identifying trends, patterns, and risk factors related to nutrition. This knowledge helps inform evidence-based decision-making and improve overall patient care.

In conclusion, technology has greatly improved the assessment of nutritional needs in individuals. From mobile applications that track dietary intake to wearable devices and body scanners that analyze body composition, technology provides more accurate, detailed, and efficient methods to evaluate and monitor nutrient requirements. Genetic testing and the use of EMRs further enhance the depth of knowledge available to healthcare professionals. The integration of technology in this aspect of healthcare not only improves patient outcomes but also enhances the overall quality of care delivered.

Personalized diets have been gaining popularity in recent years as people strive to find the most effective way to reach their health and wellness goals. By tailoring a diet to an individual's unique needs, personalized diets can offer more targeted and potentially successful results. In this article, we will explore some success stories in personalized diets and showcase how they have positively impacted people's lives.

Case Study 1: Sarah's Weight Loss Journey

Sarah had struggled with her weight for most of her adult life. She had tried numerous diets and fitness plans, but nothing seemed to provide significant and sustainable results. Frustrated, Sarah turned to a personalized diet plan recommended by a nutritionist.

Through a series of tests, including genetic analysis and comprehensive health evaluations, Sarah's nutritional needs were determined. It was discovered that she had a gene variant that made her process carbohydrates less efficiently. Armed with this information, a personalized diet plan was created, focusing on a lower carbohydrate intake and increased lean protein and healthy fats.

Over the course of several months, Sarah stuck to her personalized diet plan diligently. The results were amazing. Not only did Sarah lose weight, but she also noticed an increase in energy levels and improvements in her overall well-being. Sarah's success story highlights the importance of personalized diets in addressing specific genetic variations and tailoring them to individual needs.

Case Study 2: David's Sports Performance Enhancer

David was an avid athlete who wanted to take his performance to the next level. As he trained rigorously for a marathon, he was looking for nutritional strategies that could give him a competitive edge. David consulted a nutritionist who specialized in personalized diets for athletes.

After assessing David's nutritional needs, goals, and training regimen, a personalized diet plan was created, specifically catering to his required nutrient intake. The plan focused on optimizing carbohydrate intake to fuel his training sessions effectively, increasing his protein intake for muscle repair, and incorporating nutrient-dense foods to support his overall health.

David diligently followed his personalized diet plan and noticed significant improvements in his performance. Not only did he break his personal records during training, but he also finished the marathon with excellent timing. David's success is a testament to the efficacy of personalized diets in enhancing sports performance.

Case Study 3: Jane's Gut Health Journey

Jane had been struggling with digestive issues, including bloating, gas, and irregular bowel movements for years. She tried various diets and supplements but nothing seemed to alleviate her symptoms. Frustrated, Jane turned to a functional medicine specialist who recommended a personalized diet plan focusing on gut health.

Tests were conducted to assess Jane's gut microbiota diversity, along with food sensitivity and intolerance tests. These results were used to create an individualized diet plan that eliminated trigger foods, incorporated gut-healing foods, and included specific probiotic supplements.

After following the personalized diet plan meticulously, Jane experienced significant improvements in her digestive health. Her bloating and gas reduced, and her bowel movements became more regular. Jane's success story showcases how personalized diets can target specific health concerns and help individuals overcome long-standing issues.

From weight loss to sports performance enhancement and gut health improvement, personalized diets have shown immense potential in providing tailored solutions for individuals seeking transformative changes in their lives. These success stories highlight the importance of personalized diets in addressing individuals' unique needs and tailoring nutritional plans accordingly. With advancements in technology and research, personalized diets are likely to play an even greater role in promoting overall health and wellness in the future.

Ethical and privacy concerns have become increasingly prominent in today's digital age, particularly with the widespread use of new technologies and the collection and processing of personal data. These concerns center around the ethical implications of how data is used, and the potential violations of an individual's privacy rights.

Firstly, the collection and processing of personal data raise ethical issues regarding informed consent. Companies often collect large amounts of data from individuals without adequately informing them or giving them a choice to opt out. This raises concerns about transparency and people's rights to know how their data is being used. For instance, social media platforms may collect data on a user's browsing habits, contacts, and personal preferences to create highly targeted advertisement campaigns without the user's direct consent.

Secondly, the use of personal data for profiling and targeted advertisements has sparked ethical concerns regarding manipulation and exploitation. Companies may use personal data to create profiles of individuals, which are then used to manipulate their behavior or decisions. This manipulation can range from subtle nudging towards certain products or services, to using psychological tactics to exploit weaknesses. Such practices raise concerns about ethical implications, as individuals may unknowingly be subjected to undue influence and control.

Additionally, advances in technology have raised significant concerns about personal privacy. With the proliferation of surveillance technologies, individuals' every move can be tracked and recorded. Facial recognition technology, for example, has the potential to identify and monitor individuals without their knowledge or consent. This can lead to privacy violations and potential abuse of power by both public and private entities.

Moreover, there are concerns surrounding the security and protection of personal data. Reports of data breaches and the mismanagement of personal information are not uncommon. This puts individuals at risk of identity theft, financial fraud, and various other forms of harm. The ethical responsibility to protect personal data rests with organizations that collect and process it, but data breaches highlight the need for stronger security measures and increased accountability.

Furthermore, there are philosophical debates surrounding the ownership and control of personal data. Many argue that individuals should have control and ownership rights over their own personal data. They believe that individuals should have the right to decide who has access to their data and how it is used. However, the reality is that personal data is often collected without individuals being able to exercise control over its use.

In response to these concerns, governments and regulatory bodies have introduced legislation and guidelines to address ethical and privacy issues. For example, the General Data Protection Regulation (GDPR) in the European Union aims to strengthen data protection rights and empower individuals regarding their personal data.

In conclusion, ethical and privacy concerns surrounding the use of personal data and new technologies are of significant importance in today's digital age. Issues such as informed consent, manipulation, surveillance, data breaches, and ownership rights highlight the need for ethical guidelines and regulations to safeguard individuals' rights and protect their privacy.

Chapter 15: The Future of Seafood - Beyond Overfishing

The issue of overfishing has long plagued our oceans, putting numerous marine species at the brink of extinction and endangering the delicate balance of our marine ecosystems. However, awareness regarding overfishing and its consequences has been on the rise, leading to increased efforts to find sustainable alternatives for seafood consumption. In this chapter, we will delve into the future of seafood, exploring various innovative solutions that go beyond the current challenges of overfishing.

1. Aquaculture: The Rise of Fish Farming

One of the most promising solutions to overfishing is the development of sustainable aquaculture practices. Fish farming, or aquaculture, involves the cultivation of fish and other marine organisms in controlled environments. As technology advances, aquaculture systems are becoming increasingly efficient, reducing their impact on the marine habitat. Additionally, research is being conducted to feed farmed fish with more eco-friendly alternatives to fishmeal, such as vegetarian diets made from algae or plankton. While there are still challenges to overcome, aquaculture has the potential to alleviate the pressure on wild fish populations and provide a sustainable source of seafood.

2. Cell-Based Seafood: Growing Seafood without the Sea

A recent breakthrough in seafood innovation is the development of cell-based seafood. This process involves extracting cells from a fish or other marine organism and cultivating them in a lab to produce seafood products without the need for raising or catching actual animals. Besides offering a more ethical alternative to traditional seafood production, cell-based seafood has the potential to reduce the environmental impact associated with overfishing, such as by eliminating bycatch, habitat destruction, and pollution caused by fishing vessels.

3. Vertical Ocean Farms: Harnessing the Power of the Sun

Another exciting development in the world of sustainable seafood production is the concept of vertical ocean farms. These farms take advantage of the vast underwater space available in the ocean to cultivate a variety of seafood and seaweed. These farms use eco-friendly design principles that rely on solar energy, biomimicry, and vertical farming techniques. By harnessing the power of the sun and creating self-sustaining ecosystems, vertical ocean farms not only provide a sustainable source of seafood but also promote the restoration of marine habitats.

4. Sustainable Seafood Certification: Consumer Empowerment

As consumer awareness grows, more attention is being given to seafood sustainability certifications. Organizations like the Marine Stewardship Council (MSC) and the Aquaculture Stewardship Council (ASC) are working to certify and label seafood that meets certain sustainability criteria. These certifications allow consumers to make informed choices when purchasing seafood products, ensuring that they are supporting environmentally responsible fisheries and aquaculture practices. A widespread adoption of these certifications can incentivize the seafood industry to adopt more sustainable production methods.

5. Policy and Regulations: Protecting the Oceans

Comprehensive policies and regulations are fundamental in driving the future of sustainable seafood. Governments and international organizations play a crucial role in implementing measures to curb overfishing and promote sustainable practices. These policies can include establishing marine protected areas, setting catch limits, fostering cooperation between countries, and enforcing sustainable fishing practices through strict regulations. Effective governance and enforcement can provide a framework for the sustainable management of our oceans and encourage the transition towards a more environmentally conscious seafood industry.

Conclusion

The future of seafood holds significant promise and exciting opportunities for sustainable production methods that go beyond the challenges of overfishing. Through the development of aquaculture practices, cell-based seafood, vertical ocean farms, sustainable certifications, and robust policies and regulations, we can work towards a future where seafood consumption is no longer synonymous with environmental degradation. By embracing these innovative solutions, we can help restore the balance of our oceans and secure a bountiful future for both marine life and human societies.

The current status of global fish stocks is a subject of increasing concern. As human populations continue to grow and the demand for seafood escalates, our oceans are facing unprecedented challenges and pressures.

According to a report by the Food and Agriculture Organization of the United Nations (FAO), around 33% of the world's fish stocks are being harvested at biologically unsustainable levels. This means that these stocks are being harvested faster than they can replenish themselves through natural reproduction.

Overfishing, along with the destruction of marine habitats and pollution, has led to a decline in fish populations worldwide. It has been estimated that around 90% of large predatory fish, such as tuna, marlin, and sharks, have vanished from the oceans due to overfishing in recent decades.

Moreover, certain fishing practices like bottom trawling, where massive nets are dragged across the seabed, can cause severe damage to delicate ecosystems like coral reefs and underwater forests. This destruction affects not only the fish populations but also other marine species that depend on these habitats for survival.

Climate change is exacerbating the strain on fish stocks. Rising sea temperatures, ocean acidification, and changing currents are altering the distribution and abundance of species. For instance, many fish species are moving to cooler waters in response to rising temperatures, while others are struggling to survive in increasingly acidic environments.

The consequences of declining fish stocks extend beyond ecological concerns. Millions of people around the world rely on fish as a vital source of protein and income. In developing countries, where access to alternative food sources and livelihoods may be limited, the depletion of fish stocks can have severe socio-economic consequences.

To address this critical issue, various measures have been implemented internationally. These include the establishment of marine protected areas, the promotion of sustainable fishing practices, and the improvement of monitoring and management systems. However, more needs to be done on a global scale to reverse the decline of fish stocks and ensure the long-term sustainability of our oceans.

In conclusion, the current status of global fish stocks is cause for alarm. Overfishing, habitat destruction, pollution, and climate change have resulted in significant declines in fish populations worldwide. Urgent action is needed to conserve marine ecosystems, promote sustainable fishing practices, and secure the future availability of seafood for both ecological and socio-economic reasons.

Sustainable seafood practices are essential to ensure the long-term viability of our oceans and the livelihoods of the people who depend on them. These practices aim to protect marine ecosystems, maintain fish populations at healthy levels, and support the fishing industry in a way that contributes to the well-being of local communities.

One key aspect of sustainable seafood practices is the use of responsible fishing methods. This involves avoiding destructive methods such as bottom trawling, which can damage sensitive bottom habitats and indiscriminately catch non-target species. Instead, sustainable fisheries use more selective fishing gears, such as traps, hooks, and lines, which minimize bycatch and reduce habitat damage.

Another important component of sustainable seafood practices is the management of fish stocks. This entails setting catch limits and implementing regulations that prevent overfishing. Overfishing can deplete fish populations, disrupt the balance of marine ecosystems, and hinder the ability of fish stocks to replenish themselves. By adopting sustainable fishing practices, we can help ensure that fish populations remain abundant and can support future generations.

Regulation and monitoring play a crucial role in enforcing sustainable seafood practices. Fisheries management authorities need to establish robust monitoring systems, regularly inspect fishing activities, and enforce compliance with regulations. The use of technologies such as satellite tracking, remote sensing, and electronic monitoring systems can aid in effective monitoring and ensure that sustainable fishing practices are being followed.

Certification programs, such as the Marine Stewardship Council (MSC) and the Aquaculture Stewardship Council (ASC), also contribute to sustainable seafood practices. These programs evaluate fisheries and aquaculture operations against strict environmental, social, and economic standards. Certification provides consumers with confidence that the seafood they are purchasing has been sourced in a sustainable manner.

Educating consumers about sustainable seafood choices is also crucial for promoting sustainable practices. Labels and certifications on seafood products can help consumers make informed decisions. Additionally, engaging consumers through campaigns, educational materials, and outreach programs can raise awareness about the importance of sustainable seafood and empower individuals to make sustainable choices when shopping for seafood.

Collaboration among stakeholders, including governments, industry players, fishing communities, and conservation organizations, is essential for achieving sustainable seafood practices. By working together, these stakeholders can develop and implement effective policies, share best practices, and ensure the sustainability of our oceans for generations to come.

In conclusion, sustainable seafood practices are vital for protecting the health of our oceans and the communities that depend on them. Responsible fishing methods, effective fish stock management, regulation and monitoring, certification programs, consumer education, and collaboration are all crucial components of sustainable seafood practices. By adopting and promoting these practices, we can ensure the long-term viability of our oceans and support the livelihoods of those who rely on them.

Aquaculture, the cultivation of aquatic organisms such as fish, shellfish, and seaweed, is an industry that has seen tremendous innovation over the years. These innovations aim to improve efficiency, sustainability, and the overall productivity of aquaculture systems. In this article, we will explore some of the notable innovations in aquaculture.

One significant innovation in aquaculture is the development of recirculating aquaculture systems (RAS). Traditionally, aquaculture systems required large quantities of water and were open to the environment, which resulted in a high risk of water pollution and disease outbreaks. RAS, on the other hand, operate by treating and recirculating water within a closed system, reducing the amount of water needed as well as minimizing environmental impacts. These systems incorporate various filtration techniques to maintain water quality and can be used for a wide range of species such as fish and shrimp.

Another innovation in aquaculture is the use of genetic selection techniques to improve the performance of aquatic species. Selective breeding programs have been implemented to enhance desirable traits, such as growth rate, disease resistance, and feed conversion efficiency. This has resulted in the development of improved strains of fish and shellfish that can grow faster, require less feed, and are more resistant to diseases. Genetic selection allows for the production of healthier and more productive stocks, leading to increased yields and economic benefits.

Advancements in feed technology have also played a crucial role in transforming aquaculture. The development of nutritionally balanced and sustainable feeds has significantly reduced the industry's reliance on traditional fishmeal and fish oil, derived from wild-caught fish. New feed formulations, incorporating alternative protein sources such as plant-based proteins and microbial proteins, provide essential nutrients for fish growth, while also reducing pressure on marine resources. Additionally, the use of functional feeds, such as those rich in omega-3 fatty acids, has been explored to improve the nutritional content of farmed fish.

Automation and digitalization have also revolutionized the aquaculture industry. Innovations in sensor technology, remote monitoring systems, and machine learning algorithms allow for real-time monitoring and control of aquaculture operations. These advancements enable farmers to optimize water quality, feeding regimes, and disease detection, resulting in increased production efficiency and reduced environmental impacts. Automation can also reduce labor costs and improve worker safety, making it an attractive option for aquaculture operations.

Innovations in aquaculture are not limited to fish and shellfish production alone. Seaweed cultivation, or mariculture, has gained significant attention as a sustainable and nutrient-rich source of food and bioenergy. New technologies and cultivation methods, such as offshore seaweed farming and multi-trophic systems, have been developed to increase seaweed production and diversify its uses. Seaweeds not only absorb excess nutrients from the water, helping to mitigate eutrophication, but they can also be utilized for biofuel production, bioremediation, and even as feed additives for aquaculture species.

In conclusion, innovations in aquaculture continue to push the boundaries of sustainable and productive food production. Technologies such as recirculating aquaculture systems, genetic selection, advanced feed formulations, automation, and seaweed cultivation are transforming the industry. These innovations have the potential to improve profitability, reduce environmental impacts, and provide a reliable source of nutritious seafood for an ever-growing global population.

Plant-based and lab-grown seafood alternatives have recently gained popularity as a sustainable and ethical alternative to traditional seafood. These innovative products aim to provide the taste and texture of seafood while reducing the environmental impact of fishing and aquaculture.

Plant-based seafood alternatives are typically made from ingredients such as seaweed, algae, and other plant proteins. They are designed to mimic the taste and texture of various types of seafood, ranging from fish fillets to shrimp. These products are often perceived as a healthier option since they are typically lower in cholesterol and saturated fat compared to their animal-based counterparts.

One of the main advantages of plant-based seafood alternatives is their lower environmental footprint. Overfishing and the use of heavy fishing gear often lead to the drastic depletion of wild fish populations and the destruction of marine habitats. Plant-based alternatives offer a more sustainable solution by reducing the reliance on commercial fishing and the associated negative impacts.

Moreover, plant-based products also aim to address health concerns associated with seafood consumption. In recent years, concerns have been raised about the presence of toxins such as mercury and microplastics in seafood. Some plant-based alternatives, such as seaweed-based products, can provide a source of beneficial nutrients like omega-3 fatty acids, while avoiding these potential contaminants.

Lab-grown seafood alternatives, also known as cultured seafood, take a different approach by using cellular agriculture to grow seafood products in a controlled environment. This method involves isolating a small sample of cells from the target species and then culturing these cells in a laboratory setting to produce seafood products that are nearly identical to conventionally caught or farmed seafood.

Lab-grown seafood holds promise for solving major sustainability and ethical concerns in the seafood industry. As the global demand for seafood continues to rise, traditional fishing and aquaculture practices are unable to meet these demands sustainably. Lab-grown alternatives have the potential to generate seafood without the need for the excessive use of resources or the negative impacts on marine ecosystems.

Another benefit of lab-grown seafood is its potential to reduce the suffering of animals. Modern fishing practices often involve long periods of captivity and potentially painful capture methods for commercially important species. Lab-grown alternatives allow for the production of seafood without the need for any living animals, minimizing harm and supporting animal welfare.

While plant-based and lab-grown seafood alternatives offer promising solutions to the environmental and ethical challenges of seafood production, there are still several obstacles to overcome. These include scaling up production, ensuring affordability and availability, and gaining consumer acceptance.

As the demand for sustainable food options continues to grow, plant-based and lab-grown seafood alternatives have the potential to play a significant role in the future of our food system. These innovations offer a way to enjoy the taste of seafood while promoting a more environmentally friendly and humane approach to food production. With continued technological advancements and increased consumer awareness, the future of seafood alternatives looks promising.

Chapter 16: Food Packaging Innovations

In recent years, there has been a significant shift in the way food is packaged. With the growing concern for food safety, sustainability, and convenience, manufacturers are constantly striving to develop creative and innovative packaging solutions. This chapter explores some of the latest advancements in food packaging, ranging from the use of smart materials to biodegradable packaging options.

1. Smart Packaging

One of the most exciting developments in food packaging is the emergence of smart packaging solutions. These technologies integrate various sensors, indicators, and monitors that can detect and report information about food quality and safety. For instance, intelligent labels can change color to indicate spoilage or contamination, help regulate temperature, or even provide real-time tracking of the product's location during transportation. Such systems not only enhance the safety of food but also allow consumers to make informed decisions about the freshness and quality of the products they purchase.

2. Active Packaging

Active packaging technology involves the use of packaging materials that interact with the packaged food to improve its quality and extend shelf life. Examples of active packaging methods include the incorporation of oxygen absorbers, moisture absorbers, and antimicrobial agents. These innovations help retard the growth of microorganisms, delay oxidation processes, and prevent the degradation of nutrients, ensuring that the food stays fresher for longer. Active packaging also aids in reducing food waste by minimizing product spoilage.

3. Modified Atmosphere Packaging (MAP)

Modified Atmosphere Packaging is widely used in the food industry to maintain and extend the shelf life of perishable goods. It involves modifying the composition of the air inside the packaging by controlling the levels of oxygen, carbon dioxide, and nitrogen. By creating an atmosphere that is conducive to preserving food quality, MAP slows the growth of bacteria, fungi, and other spoilage-inducing microorganisms. This packaging technique not only enhances food safety but also minimizes the need for chemical preservatives.

4. Edible Packaging

Edible packaging has gained significant traction as a sustainable alternative to traditional packaging materials. These innovative packages are typically made from edible materials such as seaweed, starch, or gelatin. While they offer protection and containment similar to conventional packaging, edible packages break down naturally and are safe for consumption. This eco-friendly solution serves as an excellent means of reducing plastic waste, giving consumers the option to eat their packaging or discard it without worrying about the environmental impact.

5. Biodegradable and Compostable Packaging

In response to the global concern over plastic pollution, packaging manufacturers have turned their attention to developing biodegradable and compostable materials. Organic polymers derived from renewable sources like cornstarch, bamboo, and sugarcane are increasingly being used to replace conventional plastics. These biodegradable polymers are capable of breaking down naturally within a few months and pose significantly less harm to the environment. Compostable packaging further enhances sustainability as it provides nutrients to enrich soil when disposed of properly.

Conclusion

The continuous evolution of food packaging is bringing a myriad of advancements that prioritize safety, sustainability, and convenience. Smart packaging, active packaging, MAP, edible packaging, and biodegradable options are transforming the industry, improving food quality, reducing waste, and addressing environmental concerns. These innovative packaging solutions offer promising opportunities for both manufacturers and consumers as they reshape the way food is preserved, presented, and consumed.

Food packaging has a long and fascinating history, dating back thousands of years. From simple utilitarian containers to complex modern packaging materials, our methods of preserving and presenting food have evolved drastically over time.

In ancient civilizations, such as Egypt and China, food was stored and transported in simple containers made from materials such as clay or reed baskets. These containers were effective in protecting the food from external contaminants and helped to prevent spoilage. However, they did not offer extensive shelf life or preservation capabilities.

As societies developed and trade routes expanded, new methods of preserving food became necessary. The ancient Greeks and Romans used amphorae, large clay jars sealed with wax, to transport and store wine, olive oil, and other perishable goods. These vessels provided a more airtight seal, extending the lifespan of the products.

In the Middle Ages, food preservation techniques advanced with the introduction of various preservation methods. Salting, smoking, and drying became common practices to extend the shelf life of fish and meats. As packaging techniques improved, foods could be stored for longer periods, enabling exploration and international trade.

In the 19th century, the industrial revolution sparked significant developments in food packing. The invention of tin cans revolutionized the preservation and transport of food. Cans allowed for extended shelf life and protection from external contamination, making it possible to ship perishable goods across vast distances. However, tin cans were heavy, expensive, and difficult to open, limiting their widespread use.

In the early 20th century, technological advancements led to the emergence of new packaging materials. Paperboard cartons and glass bottles provided an alternative to tin cans, offering lighter weight and easier handling. These materials also allowed for clearer labeling and marketing, enabling consumers to identify and choose products more easily.

The mid-20th century marked a turning point in food packaging with the introduction of plastics. Plastic packaging offered flexibility, durability, and cost-efficiency compared to its predecessors. The discovery of polyethylene in the 1930s, followed by the development of other plastics such as polypropylene and polystyrene, paved the way for a wide range of new packaging designs and applications.

In recent decades, sustainability and environmental concerns have driven further innovation in food packaging. Advances in recyclable materials, biodegradable packaging, and compostable alternatives aim to reduce the environmental impact of packaging waste. Consumers are increasingly demanding packaging that is both functional and environmentally conscious, pushing manufacturers to explore new solutions.

In conclusion, the history of food packaging is a story of innovation, necessity, and societal advancements. From simple containers to complex materials, packaging has played a critical role in preserving and protecting food throughout the ages. As technology continues to evolve, it is likely that the future of food packaging will bring even more groundbreaking developments, shaping the way we interact with, consume, and preserve our food.

Eco-friendly and sustainable packaging solutions have gained significant traction in recent years as more businesses and consumers recognize the importance of reducing their environmental impact. These packaging solutions focus on minimizing waste, using renewable and recyclable materials, and implementing efficient manufacturing processes. In this article, we will delve into some of the key advancements and innovations in this field.

One promising approach in sustainable packaging is the use of biodegradable materials. Traditional packaging materials, such as plastics, can take hundreds or thousands of years to break down in nature, leading to considerable environmental harm. However, biodegradable materials are designed to naturally decompose, helping to protect ecosystems and reduce landfill waste.

One such material gaining popularity is bioplastics. These plastics are made from renewable resources such as corn starch, sugarcane, or vegetable oils instead of fossil fuels. Bioplastics can be used to manufacture various types of packaging, including bags, containers, and films. One of the main advantages of bioplastics is that they can be composted, reducing the burden on limited landfill space.

To further improve the sustainability of packaging, companies are also exploring alternative materials such as bamboo and mushroom-based packaging. Bamboo is a fast-growing, renewable resource that can be transformed into packaging material with minimal environmental impact. Additionally, mycelium, the root structure of mushrooms, can be used to create biodegradable packaging that is both sturdy and lightweight.

In addition to the materials used, the design and functionality of packaging are crucial in creating eco-friendly solutions. Companies are increasingly adopting minimalist designs and reducing the amount of packaging material used, which helps save resources and allows for easier disposal. Packaging designs that can be easily disassembled or reused are gaining popularity, allowing consumers to actively participate in waste reduction.

Another important aspect of sustainable packaging is the use of recycled materials. Many companies are now incorporating post-consumer recycled content into their packaging, reducing the demand for virgin materials. For instance, recycled paper and cardboard can be used to create sturdy and recyclable boxes, while recycled glass can be used for bottles and jars.

Moreover, innovative technologies are being developed to increase the efficiency of packaging production. 3D printing, for example, allows for customized packaging production, minimizing material waste by only using the necessary amount of material. This technology also reduces energy consumption and transportation emissions by enabling local production.

In conclusion, eco-friendly and sustainable packaging solutions play a critical role in reducing the environmental impact of packaging. Biodegradable materials, such as bioplastics, bamboo, and mushroom-based packaging, offer alternatives to traditional plastics, while minimalist designs and the use of recycled materials further increase sustainability. With ongoing advancements in technology and a growing consumer demand for sustainable options, the future of packaging looks set to become even more environmentally conscious.

Smart packaging refers to the integration of advanced technology into traditional product packaging, enabling these packages to provide additional functionality beyond its primary purpose of protecting and containing products. Smart packaging typically involves the use of various sensors, tracking devices, and communication technologies to enhance the packaging's capabilities.

One significant technology trend in smart packaging is the use of active and intelligent packaging. Active packaging refers to packaging that actively interacts with the product or its environment to extend shelf life or enhance the product's quality. For example, active packaging can incorporate oxygen or moisture scavengers to prevent spoilage or protect against degradation.

On the other hand, intelligent packaging focuses on providing information to the consumer or the supply chain. Intelligent packaging can include features like temperature indicators, freshness sensors, or even electronic displays to convey relevant information about the product's condition and safety.

One emerging technology in smart packaging is the use of printed electronics. Printable conductive inks with electronic properties can be used to create functional elements directly on package substrates. These elements can include sensors, antennas for wireless communication, or even power sources. Printable electronics are flexible, cost-effective, and easily incorporated into existing packaging manufacturing processes.

Another trend in smart packaging is the integration of tracking technologies like RFID (Radio-Frequency Identification) and NFC (Near Field Communication). These technologies enable real-time visibility and traceability throughout the entire supply chain. By tagging packages with RFID or NFC labels, companies can monitor inventory levels, streamline logistics, and provide accurate information to consumers.

Additionally, advancements in data analytics and cloud computing have significantly expanded the capabilities of smart packaging technology. Combined with internet connectivity, smart packaging can now transmit real-time data to cloud platforms where it can be analyzed and utilized for various purposes such as inventory management, personalized marketing, or quality control.

Moreover, smart packaging has found applications in diverse industries. In the food industry, smart packaging can ensure product freshness and safety, offering features like tamper-evident seals, temperature indicators, and quality monitoring sensors. In the healthcare sector, smart packaging can help track medication adherence or authenticate pharmaceutical products, improving patient safety and treatment effectiveness.

In conclusion, smart packaging is an evolving technology-driven concept that is transforming traditional packaging into a dynamic medium, offering enhanced functionality and value. Active and intelligent packaging, printed electronics, tracking technologies, and advanced data analytics are driving trends in this field, ushering in a new era of packaging capabilities that benefit both businesses and consumers.

As we move into the future, food packaging faces a multitude of challenges that need to be addressed. From the demand for sustainability, to the rise of e-commerce, to the increasing need for convenient and functional packaging, the future of food packaging is set to be an intriguing and complex landscape.

One of the most pressing challenges in food packaging is the demand for sustainability. With increasing awareness about environmental issues, consumers are becoming more conscious about the impact of packaging waste. Manufacturers and packaging companies are thus under pressure to find sustainable alternatives to traditional materials such as plastic.

Biodegradable and compostable packaging materials offer promising solutions to this challenge. These materials can be made from renewable resources such as plant fibers, and they break down naturally over time, reducing the amount of waste that is sent to landfills. However, there are still hurdles to overcome, such as high production costs and limited availability of such materials. Development and implementation of sustainable packaging materials will be crucial in the future.

Advancements in e-commerce have also presented challenges for food packaging. Online shopping has become increasingly popular, and this includes the purchase of perishable food items. Ensuring that these items remain fresh and intact during transportation is a critical task. Packaging that is strong enough to withstand the rigors of shipping, while also maintaining the food's quality and safety, is essential.

Packaging innovations such as insulated containers, gel packs, and vacuum-sealed bags have been developed to address these challenges. These solutions help to maintain the desired temperature and prevent contamination during transit. However, there is still room for improvement as the demand for online grocery shopping continues to increase.

Furthermore, the need for convenient and functional packaging is also on the rise. With an increasing number of people leading busy lifestyles, there is a demand for packaging that can offer convenience, such as portion control and easy-to-open designs. Additionally, as the population ages, there is a growing need for packaging that is accessible and easy to handle for people with reduced strength or mobility.

Packaging companies are responding to these demands by developing innovative packaging designs. For example, resealable pouches, portion-controlled packaging, and easy-open lids are becoming more prevalent. These advancements not only cater to the needs of consumers but also aim to reduce food waste by offering convenient storage solutions.

Another challenge that must be addressed in the future of food packaging is the issue of food safety. Ensuring that food is packaged in a way that preserves its freshness and prevents contamination is of utmost importance. This includes considerations such as barrier properties, oxygen absorption, and moisture control.

Many packaging companies are investing in technologies such as active and intelligent packaging solutions. Active packaging actively interacts with the food to extend shelf life, while intelligent packaging provides real-time information about the quality and safety of the product. By incorporating these technologies, food packaging can play a vital role in maintaining food safety standards.

In conclusion, the future of food packaging is filled with challenges and opportunities. From the emphasis on sustainability to the rise of e-commerce and the need for convenience, packaging companies must adapt and innovate to meet the evolving demands of consumers. By developing sustainable materials, addressing the unique requirements of e-commerce, delivering convenient and functional designs, and ensuring food safety, the industry can overcome these challenges and create a promising future for food packaging.

Chapter 17: The Social Aspect of Food

Food is not only a basic necessity for our survival; it also plays a significant role in our social lives. The act of eating together has long been regarded as a fundamental element of human culture and society. In this chapter, we will delve deeper into the social aspect of food and explore its various dimensions.

1. Food as a Cultural Symbol:

Food is deeply intertwined with cultural identity around the world. Different societies attach specific meanings and symbols to various types of food, which can vary based on region, religion, or even individual beliefs. For example, pork holds different significance for Jews, Muslims, and non-religious individuals. Exploring these cultural symbols helps us understand how food acts as a conduit for expressing and preserving cultural traditions.

2. Food and Communal Identity:

Sharing a meal with others fosters a sense of belonging and strengthens communal bonds. Whether it is during family dinners, religious celebrations, or community feasts, the act of sitting at a table and eating together creates a shared experience that goes beyond just nourishment. Through food, we connect with others on multiple levels – emotionally, socially, and spiritually.

3. Food and Social Class:

Our choices of food often reflect our social statuses and aspirations. Food can be used to signal class distinctions, with certain cuisines and ingredients associated with wealth and prestige. Additionally, differences in access to quality food and dietary choices can create a social divide, impacting the overall health and well-being of individuals within a society.

4. Food and Celebrations:

Throughout history, food has played a central role in celebrations and special occasions. Whether it's a birthday, wedding, or festival, the right food can elevate the atmosphere and create a memorable experience. Specific dishes or ingredients are often synonymous with certain festivities and are eagerly anticipated by all. The act of coming together to indulge in these culinary delights enhances the joy and bonding that accompanies these events.

5. Food and Social Norms:

Food is profoundly influenced by social norms and expectations. These norms dictate not only what should be consumed but also the ways in which it should be prepared, served, and eaten. Cultural etiquette governs dining practices, such as the use of utensils, seating arrangements, and acceptable behaviors at the table. Failure to conform to these norms can often lead to social judgment and ostracization.

6. Food and Social Exchange:

Food can also serve as a symbolic exchange within society. Hospitality is often demonstrated by offering food to guests, but it can also represent power and influence. Feeding others can imply charity, gratitude, or a display of abundance. Cultural practices like potluck dinners, communal cooking, and food-sharing initiatives all exemplify how food can be a mechanism for social exchange.

FOOD IS NOT JUST SUSTENANCE; it is a complex social construct that influences and reflects our connections with others. It acts as a powerful tool for cultural expression, community building, and social bonding. By recognizing the social aspect of food, we gain a deeper appreciation for the significance it holds in our lives beyond mere nourishment.

Food has long been recognized as a cultural connector, a medium through which people can come together and share their heritage, traditions, and stories. Whether it's a family gathering, a community event, or a celebratory feast, food plays a central role in bringing people together and fostering a sense of belonging.

One of the most evident ways in which food serves as a cultural connector is through the traditional recipes and cooking methods handed down through generations. These recipes not only convey a particular taste but also hold the history and traditions of a particular culture. From Italian pasta sauces simmered for hours, to Indian curries infused with a medley of spices, to Mexican salsas packed with fresh ingredients, these traditional dishes act as a nostalgic link to the past and provide a sense of identity to those who prepare and consume them.

Food festivals and culinary events also play a significant role in connecting people from different cultures. These events provide a platform for showcasing the diverse array of cuisines and cooking techniques from around the world. People of all backgrounds have the opportunity to come together and experience various flavors, aromas, and textures. Food festivals often offer a chance to engage with and learn from the chefs and cooks who graciously share their culinary knowledge and expertise.

Furthermore, the role of food in religious and spiritual practices cannot be overlooked. Many religious rituals involve certain types of food or specific ways of preparing meals. For example, during the Hindu festival of Diwali, families prepare elaborate feasts with special sweets and snacks that are shared with loved ones and offered to the deities. Similarly, in the Jewish tradition, families gather for the Passover Seder, where specific foods symbolize the journey from slavery to freedom. These religious traditions create a deep sense of unity and provide a shared experience that goes beyond mere sustenance.

Additionally, the sharing of meals and food-related activities fosters social connectivity and bonding among individuals. Eating together is often associated with sharing stories, laughter, and friendship. It provides an opportunity for people to connect on a deeper level, to understand and appreciate each other's backgrounds, and to build lasting relationships. The act of breaking bread together has a powerful effect on bringing people together, transcending barriers of culture, language, and geography.

In today's multicultural society, the importance of food as a cultural connector has become even more significant. As people from diverse backgrounds coexist in the same communities, food serves as a bridge, allowing individuals to share their culture and traditions, learn from one another, and celebrate their differences. It encourages inclusivity, education, and openness, fostering a sense of belonging and understanding.

In conclusion, food holds a special place in our lives as a cultural connector. It brings people together, preserves cultural traditions, heightens societal and religious practices, and strengthens our sense of belonging. Food is not merely sustenance; it is a vehicle that carries the stories, memories, and heritage of our diverse world.

Social dining trends and practices have evolved significantly over the years, reflecting changes in social norms, cultural influences, and technological advancements. In today's fast-paced and hyper-connected society, dining is more than just a means of sustenance; it has become a medium for socializing, celebrating, and forging relationships.

One major trend in social dining is the shift towards communal dining experiences. Instead of having individual tables separated by partitions, many restaurants and eateries now offer communal tables where different groups of diners can sit together. This trend, inspired by the concept of community dining, aims to create a more inclusive and sociable atmosphere where people can interact with strangers and have meaningful conversations. Communal dining not only promotes a sense of togetherness but also allows diners to share their food experiences, recommend dishes, and engage in culinary discussions.

Another emerging trend is the practice of hosting pop-up dinners and supper clubs. These events, typically organized by chefs or aspiring culinary enthusiasts, offer unique dining experiences in unconventional locations. Pop-up dinners often have limited seating, creating an intimate setting that encourages diners to interact with each other and the chef. These experiences often showcase creative menus, experimental cooking techniques, and unusual food pairings, attracting food enthusiasts and adventure-seekers who crave novel culinary experiences.

Furthermore, social media has revolutionized the way we engage with food and dining. With the rise of platforms like Instagram and Pinterest, food porn has become a widespread phenomenon. Diners are increasingly seeking aesthetically appealing and Instagram-worthy dishes that not only satisfy their taste buds but also look visually stunning. This has led to an emphasis on food presentation and garnishes, as chefs and restaurateurs recognize the power of social media in promoting their culinary creations. Social media has also become a platform for sharing dining experiences, restaurant reviews, and recommendations, providing a sense of connection and community among food enthusiasts.

Vegetarian and plant-based eating has also gained significant momentum in recent years. Whether it's due to health concerns, ethical reasons, or environmental consciousness, an increasing number of people are opting for vegetarian or vegan diets. Consequently, restaurants and food establishments have adapted to this trend by offering vegetarian-friendly menus and plant-based alternatives to classic dishes. Additionally, vegetarianism has transcended its hippie stereotype and is now embraced by individuals from all walks of life, making it easier for vegetarians and vegans to find dining options that suit their preferences.

Technological advances have also had a profound impact on social dining practices. Online reservation systems, mobile apps, and food delivery services have streamlined the dining experience, offering convenience and accessibility for diners. People can now browse menus, reserve tables, and even order food from the comfort of their homes. These technological tools have not only enhanced the efficiency of the dining process but also allowed for personalized dining experiences, as customers can tailor their orders and preferences. Furthermore, technology has enabled remote social dining experiences, where friends and family from different locations can gather virtually to dine together via video calls or livestreams, fostering a sense of connection despite physical distances.

In conclusion, social dining trends and practices have evolved significantly due to changing social dynamics, cultural influences, and technological advancements. Communal dining, pop-up dinners, social media, vegetarianism, and technology have all played crucial roles in enhancing the inclusivity, engagement, and convenience of dining experiences. As society continues to evolve, it is likely that these trends will further evolve to meet the ever-changing needs and desires of diners.

Food plays a major role in today's social media and influencer culture. With countless individuals documenting their every bite and food establishments vying for attention, the world of food in social media has become a booming industry in its own right. From Instagrammable dishes to tantalizing recipe videos, food content has taken over various social media platforms, influencing our food choices and shaping our dining experiences.

Food on social media is no longer simply about sustenance; it has evolved into a form of art, with vibrant and visually appealing dishes taking center stage. Influencers tastefully arrange mouth-watering meals for their followers who crave a feast for the eyes. The advent of filters, angles, and various editing tools has allowed food photography to flourish, making even a simple bowl of cereal look like a work of art. And with hashtags like #FoodPorn and #Foodie, food content creators find it easier than ever to reach an audience that craves indulgence and seeks jaw-dropping visuals.

Influencers play a crucial role in shaping our perception of food. Their thoughtful captions, restaurant recommendations, and recipe ideas help us decide where to dine and what to cook. We look to them as reliable sources for inspiration, authenticity, and credible reviews, leading to our increased reliance on social media when it comes to important culinary choices.

Not only do influencers influence our food choices, but they also hold sway over food establishments. Restaurants eager for positive exposure cultivate relationships with influential individuals, offering them free meals or exclusive experiences to showcase their establishments to a wider audience. A well-crafted post or a mention from a trusted influencer can drive traffic and elevate a venue's popularity overnight, leading to increased revenue and an expanded customer base.

However, the influence of social media on food extends beyond visually appealing dishes and positive reviews. It has also contributed to the rise of food trends. Remember the cronut? What about kale chips? From avocado toast to rainbow bagels, social media has propelled food trends into the mainstream consciousness, triggering viral sensations and turning ordinary foods into culinary obsessions. These trends may come and go, but they leave a lasting mark on both our taste buds and cultural memory.

Nonetheless, the impact of food in social media and influencer culture is not without its criticisms. Many argue that the obsession with picture-perfect dishes encourages an unhealthy relationship with food, promoting appearance over taste and diminishing the appreciation for home-cooked meals. Social media's influence on our food choices has also been accused of homogenizing culinary experiences, as unique regional cuisines are often overshadowed by the viral and uniform trends dominating our screens.

Despite these concerns, there is no denying the allure of food in social media and influencer culture. It has revolutionized the way we see, experience, and consume our meals. Food photography has become an art form, and influencers have assumed the role of culinary tastemakers. As we scroll through our feeds, the creativity, deliciousness, and cultural significance that food embodies entice and captivate us, ensuring that food in social media and influencer culture will continue to leave a lasting impact on our tastes and experiences.

Food festivals and events showcase the rich diversity of culinary traditions from around the world. These celebrations are not only an opportunity for people to indulge in delicious food but also a chance to learn about different cultures and their gastronomic heritage. With a wide range of flavors, cooking techniques, and ingredients on display, food festivals have become popular attractions for tourists and locals alike.

One such renowned event is the Taste of Chicago, held annually in the Windy City. This culinary extravaganza attracts food enthusiasts from near and far, offering a wide array of delectable treats. From deep-dish pizzas to Chicago-style hot dogs, attendees can sample iconic dishes that define the city's food scene. Additionally, the festival features live cooking demonstrations by renowned chefs, providing valuable insights into their craft.

Moving across the globe, Japan is home to numerous unique food festivals. One standout event is the Sapporo Snow Festival, celebrating winter cuisine in Hokkaido. During the festival, vendors line the streets, serving up piping hot bowls of ramen, fresh sushi, and grilled seafood. Visitors can also indulge in regional delicacies like Jingisukan, a popular grilled mutton dish. As the festival takes place during Japan's snowy season, attendees can enjoy their food while appreciating stunning ice sculptures and snow art.

In Europe, the city of Bologna, Italy, hosts the FICO Eataly World event, a food festival dedicated to regional Italian cuisine. With over forty culinary stations, visitors can sample authentic traditional dishes from each of Italy's regions. From creamy risotto from Lombardy to Neapolitan-style pizza and creamy gelato from Sicily, every region's gastronomic wonders are on display. Additionally, interactive workshops and talks are held to educate participants about the history and techniques behind these iconic dishes.

Venturing further east, the Mulu Indigenous Food and Craft Festival in Borneo, Malaysia, showcases the unique flavors of the indigenous communities. Here, visitors can experience traditional cooking methods like bamboo cooking and taste ancient recipes passed down through generations. The festival promotes local ingredients and culinary traditions while fostering sustainable practices to preserve the region's cultural heritage.

Food festivals and events are not limited to showcasing local cuisine; they also celebrate international flavors. The World Gourmet Summit in Singapore is a prime example of an event bridging different culinary cultures. This prestigious festival invites renowned chefs from around the world to curate extraordinary dining experiences. Attendees can savor dishes from Michelin-starred restaurants as well as street food stalls, all highlighting the global culinary kaleidoscope.

Overall, food festivals and events worldwide offer a delicious and enlightening experience for food lovers. These gatherings provide a platform for cultures to come together through their shared love for food. Whether enjoying traditional dishes, exploring street food markets, or learning new cooking techniques, attendees leave with not only satisfied palates but also a broader understanding and appreciation of the world's diverse gastronomic tapestry.

Chapter 18: Food Security and Global Challenges

In today's rapidly changing world, ensuring global food security has become an increasingly complex challenge. With a growing world population, changing dietary patterns, climate change, and natural resource limitations, the need for sustainable and resilient food systems has never been more urgent. This chapter explores the multiple dimensions of food security and the global challenges involved in achieving it.

Defining Food Security:

Food security is a condition in which all people, at all times, have physical, social, and economic access to safe, sufficient, and nutritious food that meets their dietary needs and food preferences for an active and healthy life. It encompasses four main dimensions: availability, access, utilization, and stability.

Availability: Adequate food production is essential for food security. This involves both domestic production and access to international markets. Factors such as climate change, land degradation, and water scarcity can significantly impact food availability.

Access: In addition to availability, access to food is crucial. It involves the ability to afford, obtain, and consume food. Socioeconomic factors such as income inequality, unemployment, and high food prices can limit people's access to nutritious food.

Utilization: Ensuring access to food is not enough; it must also be of good quality and provide proper nutrition. Factors such as education, health services, and sanitation play a vital role in ensuring proper food utilization, especially for vulnerable groups like children and pregnant women.

Stability: Food security requires stable access to food over time. Stability can be threatened by natural disasters, political unrest, and economic shocks. Building resilience in food systems is necessary to mitigate risks and ensure long-term food security.

Global Challenges:

1. Population Growth: The world population is projected to reach 9.7 billion by 2050, requiring a significant increase in food production. Balancing population growth with limited natural resources poses substantial challenges in meeting future food demand.

2. Climate Change: Rising global temperatures, erratic rainfall patterns, and extreme weather events are impacting agricultural productivity and food production. Climate change adaptation and mitigation strategies are imperative to protect crop yields and maintain food security.

3. Land and Water Scarcity: Shrinking arable land and decreasing freshwater availability pose significant challenges to agricultural production. Sustainable land management practices, efficient irrigation techniques, and water conservation efforts are required to optimize resource use and protect food security.

4. Poverty and Inequality: Poverty and food insecurity often go hand in hand. Income disparities, lack of access to productive resources, and limited social safety nets contribute to food insecurity. Addressing poverty and inequality is crucial to improving food security globally.

5. Changing Diets: Rapid urbanization, increased affluence, and cultural shifts are driving changes in dietary patterns. The shift towards resource-intensive diets, such as meat-heavy diets, puts additional pressure on resource use and exacerbates environmental challenges. Encouraging sustainable and healthy diets is essential for long-term food security.

ACHIEVING GLOBAL FOOD security in the face of numerous challenges remains a paramount task. Addressing the multidimensional nature of food security demands comprehensive strategies that incorporate sustainable agricultural practices, improved access to resources, poverty reduction measures, climate change adaptation, and a shift towards sustainable diets. Collaboration between governments, international organizations, civil society, and the private sector is crucial to meeting this global challenge and ensuring a future where everyone has access to safe, sufficient, and nutritious food.

Food security is a complex issue that affects people all around the world. It refers to the availability, access, and utilization of food to ensure that all individuals have enough to eat and can maintain a healthy and active lifestyle. In this article, we will delve into the topic of food security, understanding its various dimensions and the challenges that hinder its achievement.

One of the main dimensions of food security is food availability. This refers to the physical quantity of food present in a given area. It involves factors such as agricultural production, imports, and food stocks. A region with high food availability has a greater likelihood of meeting the food demands of its population. However, it is important to note that simply having food available in large quantities does not guarantee food security. It also needs to be accessible to the population.

Food accessibility is another critical dimension of food security. It encompasses economic, social, and physical barriers that prevent individuals from obtaining sufficient food. Economic barriers include factors such as high food prices, inadequate income, or lack of employment opportunities. Social barriers may include discrimination, lack of education or awareness about nutritious food, or cultural practices that restrict access to certain types of food. Physical barriers refer to geographical or infrastructural limitations that hinder the transport of food to and within a particular region. For example, remote areas or conflict zones may face challenges in accessing food.

Even if food is available and accessible, it is essential to ensure that it is utilized properly to contribute to food security. This dimension of food security is known as food utilization. It involves factors such as food safety, nutritional content, and cultural acceptability. Food safety refers to the absence of contaminants or harmful substances that can cause illness or health problems. Nutritional content focuses on the quality and adequacy of the nutrients present in the food. A diverse and balanced diet is crucial for maintaining good health. Moreover, cultural acceptability refers to the alignment of available food with local dietary preferences and traditions.

Food security is a global concern, and achieving it is an ongoing challenge. Several factors contribute to the achievement of food security, such as agricultural productivity, efficient distribution systems, and strong governance. However, a number of challenges hinder the realization of food security in various parts of the world.

Climate change poses a significant threat to food security. Rising temperatures, changing weather patterns, and increased occurrences of extreme weather events can negatively impact agricultural productivity. Droughts, floods, and heatwaves can lead to crop failures, livestock losses, and disrupted food production. Climate change also affects freshwater availability, which is essential for irrigation and farming. Without adequate water resources, farmers struggle to produce enough food to meet demands.

Conflict and political instability are other major challenges to food security. In regions affected by armed conflicts or political crises, food production and distribution systems are often disrupted. Farming activities are abandoned due to insecurity, and infrastructure necessary for the transportation of food is damaged or destroyed. In such situations, people are unable to access sufficient food, leading to high levels of hunger and malnutrition.

Another challenge is the unequal distribution of resources and power. In many societies, food is not distributed equitably. Some individuals or groups have greater access to resources, while others face food insecurity and poverty. This unequal distribution can result from factors such as social inequalities, ineffective policies, and corruption. Addressing these disparities and ensuring fair and equitable distribution of resources are crucial steps towards achieving food security.

In conclusion, food security is a complex issue that involves multiple dimensions and faces numerous challenges. Ensuring availability, accessibility, and utilization of food is essential to meet the basic needs of individuals and communities. Key challenges like climate change, conflict, and unequal resource distribution need to be addressed at local, national, and global levels to achieve sustainable food security for all.

Global Initiatives and Policies on Food Security have gained significant attention in recent years due to the rising concerns over food scarcity and malnutrition worldwide. Governments, international organizations, and non-governmental organizations (NGOs) are all actively involved in formulating policies and implementing initiatives to tackle this complex issue. In this article, we will explore some of the key Global Initiatives and Policies on Food Security, their objectives, and the strategies employed to achieve them.

The United Nations' Sustainable Development Goals (SDGs) serve as a cornerstone for many global initiatives and policies on food security. SDG 2 - Zero Hunger - specifically targets the elimination of hunger, malnutrition, and food insecurity by 2030. Under this goal, the four main objectives include ending hunger, achieving food security, improving nutrition, and promoting sustainable agriculture. The SDGs provide a framework for countries to align their policies and prioritize actions to address these pressing challenges.

One of the significant global initiatives aimed at improving food security is the World Food Programme (WFP). As the largest humanitarian agency fighting hunger around the world, WFP provides assistance to millions of people in need. It focuses on emergency response, nutrition programs, school feeding initiatives, and support for small-scale farmers. Moreover, WFP collaborates with governments, NGOs, and private sector partners to strengthen food systems and build resilience to shocks.

Another critical global initiative is the Food and Agriculture Organization (FAO), a specialized agency of the United Nations. FAO's mandate is to achieve a world without hunger by tackling issues related to agriculture, fisheries, and forestry. FAO provides technical assistance, promotes sustainable farming practices, and supports countries in their policymaking processes. One of FAO's flagship programs is the Voluntary Guidelines on the Right to Food, which provides guidelines and recommendations for countries concerning their obligation to respect, protect, and fulfill the right to adequate food.

Regional initiatives also play a crucial role in addressing food security challenges. For example, the African Union has established the Comprehensive Africa Agriculture Development Programme (CAADP). Through CAADP, African countries collaborate to unlock the potential of agriculture by investing in sectors such as irrigation, agribusiness, and rural infrastructure. It places an emphasis on sustainable agricultural growth and increased productivity to ensure food security on the continent.

At the national level, countries implement various policies to improve food security. For instance, some countries focus on increasing agricultural productivity through investment in research and development, technology transfer, and modernizing farming techniques. Others prioritize social protection programs that target vulnerable populations, ensuring their access to nutritious and affordable food. Some countries also strive to diversify their agricultural systems and promote crops that are resilient to climate change to reduce the impact of climate variability on food production.

To achieve the goals of global initiatives and policies on food security, many strategies are employed. These strategies include improving rural infrastructure such as roads and irrigation systems to enhance agricultural productivity and facilitate the movement of goods. Enhancing access to credit and finance for small-scale farmers helps them invest in their farms and improve productivity. Promoting agricultural extension services and providing technical assistance to farmers enables them to adopt modern technologies and best practices. Strengthening market systems and ensuring fair prices for agricultural products also contribute to improving food security.

In conclusion, Global Initiatives and Policies on Food Security are comprehensive and multifaceted. They encompass actions and strategies at the international, regional, and national levels to eliminate hunger, improve nutrition, and promote sustainable agriculture. These initiatives aim to address the root causes of food insecurity while building resilience to ensure the availability and access to nutritious and affordable food for all.

Technology has played a vital role in improving food security around the world. With the global population rapidly increasing and resources becoming scarcer, there is a growing need to find innovative ways to produce and distribute food more efficiently and sustainably. Fortunately, advancements in technology have made significant contributions to ensuring a stable and secure food supply for people across the globe.

One area where technology has had a significant impact on food security is in agricultural practices. Traditional farming methods often rely on large amounts of land, water, and chemicals to produce crops. However, with the advent of precision agriculture, farmers can now use technology to optimize their planting and harvesting processes. By leveraging data obtained through satellites, drones, and sensors, farmers can monitor soil moisture, nutrient levels, and plant health in real-time. This allows them to make informed decisions about when and where to apply fertilizers, pesticides, and water, minimizing waste and maximizing yield. This not only reduces costs for farmers but also reduces the environmental impact of agriculture.

Furthermore, technology has also revolutionized crop breeding and genetic engineering, contributing to improved crop yields and resilience. Through genetic modification, scientists have been able to develop crops that are resistant to diseases, pests, and harsh climatic conditions. These genetically modified crops have the potential to greatly enhance food security, especially in regions prone to droughts, floods, or extreme temperature fluctuations that can destroy entire harvests. Additionally, technology has made it easier and faster to identify valuable traits in crops and cross-pollinate them, leading to the creation of high-yielding, disease-resistant varieties.

In addition to agricultural practices, technology has also played a crucial role in enhancing the storage and distribution of food. Transportation and storage infrastructure can often be inadequate in developing countries, resulting in spoilage and significant post-harvest losses. However, technological innovations such as refrigeration, cold chains, and improved packaging have helped extend the shelf life of produce and minimize food waste. Moreover, advancements in logistics and supply chain management, including digital traceability systems, have made it easier to track and monitor the movement of food from farms to markets. This not only improves food safety but also reduces the risk of food fraud or contamination.

Furthermore, technology has facilitated better access to market information. The advent of mobile technology and internet connectivity has made it possible for farmers to access real-time market prices, weather forecasts, and other valuable information. This knowledge enables them to make informed decisions about when and where to sell their produce, ensuring better returns on their investments and reducing post-harvest losses. Moreover, technologies such as mobile payment platforms and e-commerce have opened up new avenues for farmers to directly sell their products to consumers and bypass intermediaries, leading to more equitable prices and greater market access.

While technology has undoubtedly made significant contributions to improving food security, it is essential to ensure that all individuals, especially small-scale farmers and marginalized communities, have access to and can benefit from these advancements. Governments, international organizations, and other stakeholders should work collaboratively to bridge the digital divide and provide training and resources to enable everyone to leverage the potential of technology in the agricultural sector. Additionally, the ethical and environmental considerations associated with certain technological interventions should be carefully assessed to ensure that they are safe, sustainable, and equitable.

In conclusion, technology has played a crucial role in improving food security by optimizing agricultural practices, enhancing crop breeding and genetic engineering, improving storage and distribution processes, and facilitating better access to market information. These advancements have not only increased food production and availability but have also enhanced the resilience and sustainability of our food systems. However, it is essential to ensure that technology is accessible, inclusive, and used responsibly to maximize its potential in addressing food security challenges globally.

In recent years, the future of various industries has been under constant scrutiny and speculation due to the rapid advancements in technology and changing consumer behaviors. The same can be said for the field of business strategy. As companies strive to stay innovative and competitive in an increasingly global marketplace, the development of future strategies and addressing potential challenges becomes paramount. In this regard, it is essential for business leaders to identify and understand the key aspects related to future strategies and challenges for their organizations.

A major factor that will shape future strategies is the ongoing technological revolution. Technologies such as artificial intelligence, machine learning, and big data analytics are transforming industries and disrupting traditional business models. Companies need to acknowledge and leverage these technologies to gain a competitive edge. Strategic planning should involve investing in research and development to develop new technologies, software, and products to remain ahead of the curve.

Furthermore, the growing emphasis on sustainability and corporate social responsibility will significantly impact future business strategies. Consumer preferences have shifted towards environmentally-friendly practices, ethically-sourced products, and socially-conscious organizations. Businesses must place great emphasis on embracing sustainable practices and implementing social responsibility programs to attract and retain customers. This could involve investing in renewable energy, reducing carbon footprints, adopting waste management strategies, and engaging in philanthropic pursuits.

The digital revolution has also brought about new marketing channels, and therefore, companies need to embrace digital marketing strategies to effectively engage with customers. Online advertising, social media marketing, influencer partnerships, and personalized marketing are all avenues that need to be explored in order to capture target audiences.

As organizations strive to remain relevant, they must also tackle various challenges that lie ahead. Prolonged economic uncertainties, geopolitical instabilities, and changing regulatory landscapes introduce significant complexities for companies. Strategic planning should assess these challenges and devise contingency plans to mitigate potential risks and ensure continuity of operations.

Another challenge that businesses currently face is the rise of data security threats and cyber-attacks. The sensitive customer and organizational data gathered need to be effectively safeguarded against unauthorized access or breaches to protect the goodwill of the organization. Companies should invest in robust cybersecurity measures and regularly update their systems to stay on top of emerging threats.

Lastly, the changing workforce landscape will require companies to adapt their strategies. As more remote work opportunities emerge, businesses need to be flexible in their workforce policies and establish effective remote working infrastructure. Furthermore, attracting and retaining top-talent becomes crucial for the future prospects of an organization. Company cultures must be conducive to the needs and aspirations of the modern workforce to ensure productivity and success.

In conclusion, crafting future strategies must take into account the ongoing technological revolution, growing sustainability concerns, and the need for effective digital marketing. Businesses should also be prepared to face and overcome challenges such as economic uncertainties, geopolitical instabilities, data security threats, and evolving workforce dynamics. By proactively addressing these factors and continuously adapting, organizations can position themselves for success in an ever-changing business landscape.

Chapter 19: Culinary Education and Career Trends

In recent years, the culinary industry has experienced a significant transformation, leading to renewed interest in culinary education and a shift in career trends. With a growing appreciation for diverse culinary traditions and an increasing demand for innovative culinary experiences, individuals are now more inclined to pursue culinary education as a means to thrive in this evolving industry. This chapter aims to explore the current trends in culinary education, shedding light on the various educational pathways available, and forecasting the future of culinary careers.

The Evolution of Culinary Education:

Traditional culinary education primarily focused on the techniques and fundamentals of cooking, with classical French cuisine as the cornerstone. However, as the culinary landscape changed, so did the curriculum. Today, culinary education has evolved to include a much broader range of cuisines, culinary arts, and hospitality management.

Culinary Institutes and Hospitality Schools:

Culinary institutes and hospitality schools remain prominent in the culinary education landscape. These institutions offer comprehensive programs that cover everything from basic culinary skills to advanced techniques, food business management, and even entrepreneurship. Examples of renowned culinary institutes include the French Culinary Institute, Culinary Institute of America, and Le Cordon Bleu.

Culinary Arts Programs in Colleges and Universities:

Beyond specialized culinary institutes and hospitality schools, many colleges and universities now offer culinary arts programs as part of their curriculum. These programs often provide a more comprehensive education, combining practical training with coursework in areas such as nutrition, food science, and menu planning. Culinary arts degrees are becoming increasingly recognized in the industry, offering a broader skill set for aspiring culinary professionals.

Online and Hybrid Culinary Education:

In recent years, the accessibility of culinary education has expanded significantly with the advent of online learning platforms. Online culinary schools and programs have gained popularity, providing flexibility and personalized learning experiences to students worldwide. These programs often offer video demonstrations, interactive assignments, and virtual cooking labs, allowing students to learn and practice their culinary skills remotely.

Shift Towards Sustainable and Plant-Based Education:

With the growing concerns regarding climate change and sustainability, there has been a noticeable shift towards sustainable culinary education. Many culinary schools are integrating sustainable practices into their curriculum, teaching students about responsible sourcing, reducing food waste, and implementing eco-friendly techniques. Additionally, there is a rise in plant-based culinary education, as more people opt for vegetarian and vegan diets. Culinary schools are now offering specialized courses in plant-based cooking, exploring the use of alternative ingredients and innovative cooking techniques.

Career Trends in the Culinary Industry:

The culinary industry is witnessing a transformation in career trends, influenced by evolving consumer preferences and changing market dynamics. Here are a few noteworthy career trends in the culinary world:

1. Pop-Up Restaurants and Food Trucks:

In recent years, pop-up restaurants and food trucks have gained immense popularity, offering a unique dining experience and allowing chefs to experiment with their culinary skills without the substantial investment of a brick-and-mortar establishment. This trend allows culinary professionals to explore different cuisines and concepts while catering to a diverse clientele.

2. Farm-to-Table and Locally Sourced Cuisine:

The farm-to-table movement has gained significant momentum, with an increasing emphasis on locally sourced ingredients and sustainable farming practices. Chefs and culinary professionals committed to this trend work closely with local farmers and suppliers to create seasonal dishes that highlight the flavors and freshness of regional produce.

3. Food Media and Influencer Culture:

With the rise of social media and food-focused platforms, the food media industry has experienced tremendous growth. Culinary influencers, bloggers, and food photographers are now coveted tastemakers, shaping consumer trends and driving culinary conversations. This trend has created new career opportunities as individuals pursue careers in digital marketing, food writing, recipe development, and food photography.

4. Non-Traditional Culinary Careers:

While the restaurant industry continues to be a popular career path, there is an increasing number of culinary professionals venturing into non-traditional careers. Some examples include culinary consultants, personal chefs, private caterers, food stylists, and culinary instructors. These diverse career paths allow culinary professionals to showcase their skills in unique ways and cater to a wide range of clients and customers.

AS THE CULINARY INDUSTRY evolves, culinary education and career trends follow suit, providing a myriad of opportunities for aspiring chefs and culinary professionals. With a focus on sustainability, innovation, and diversification, individuals are finding new ways to excel in their culinary careers, contributing to the vibrant and ever-changing landscape of the culinary world. Whether through traditional culinary institutes, online culinary programs, or non-traditional career paths, culinary education and careers are embracing the dynamic needs of the industry and shaping its future.

Culinary education has come a long way over the years. The field has evolved significantly, with new techniques, tools, and ingredients being introduced all the time. This evolution has resulted in a need for culinary education to keep up with the changing times.

In the past, culinary education was often seen as a trade that could be learned through hands-on experience. Many chefs learned their skills through apprenticeships or by working their way up in the kitchen. While this approach certainly taught them the basics of cooking, it didn't necessarily give them a broader understanding of the culinary industry as a whole. They usually only mastered the skills needed for one specific type of cuisine or cooking style.

However, as the culinary industry began to grow and diversify, the need for a more formalized education became apparent. This led to the establishment of culinary schools and programs that offered a more comprehensive curriculum. Students could now learn everything from classical French techniques to new fusion cuisines.

The curriculum in culinary schools shifted to include not only cooking techniques but also nutrition, food safety, menu planning, and business management. These additions were necessary to prepare students for the demands of a modern culinary career. It was no longer enough to simply know how to cook; chefs needed to understand how to run a successful kitchen and create dishes that were nutritious and appealing to a variety of diners.

At the same time, the development of new technologies and techniques in the culinary world also played a role in the evolution of culinary education. The introduction of molecular gastronomy, for example, brought a whole new set of skills and knowledge that had to be incorporated into the curriculum. Chefs needed to understand the chemistry behind these techniques in order to create innovative and exciting dishes.

As the demand for diverse cuisines grew, culinary schools began offering specialized programs in areas such as pastry and baking, international cuisines, and hospitality management. This allowed aspiring chefs to focus on their specific interest and it also opened up new career opportunities in the industry.

Today, culinary education has taken yet another turn with the advent of online learning platforms. Chefs and culinary experts from around the world can now share their knowledge and skills through virtual classes and interactive tutorials. This accessibility to information has made culinary education more accessible to aspiring chefs who may not have the means to attend a traditional culinary school.

Furthermore, the COVID-19 pandemic has accelerated the development of online culinary education. As in-person classes became impossible, culinary schools were forced to adapt and embrace online learning methods. This shift has not only allowed aspiring chefs to continue their education but has also created new opportunities for chefs to share their expertise and monetize their skills through online cooking classes and demonstrations.

In conclusion, the evolution of culinary education has been a response to the changing demands and trends of the culinary industry. From hands-on experience to formalized education, culinary schools have become more comprehensive in their curriculum, covering not only cooking techniques but also menu planning, food safety, and business management. The development of new technologies and techniques has also influenced culinary education, requiring chefs to learn about molecular gastronomy and other innovative approaches. Online learning platforms have further widened access to culinary education, allowing aspiring chefs to learn from experts worldwide. The evolution of culinary education is ongoing, and it will continue to adapt as the culinary world continues to progress and innovate.

The food industry is a bustling and highly competitive field that encompasses a wide range of careers and opportunities. From chefs and restaurant owners to food scientists and nutritionists, there has always been a demand for skilled professionals in this industry.

But with advancements in technology, changes in consumer preferences, and a greater emphasis on sustainability and health, new career paths are emerging in the food industry. These emerging career paths offer exciting opportunities for individuals who are passionate about food and are willing to adapt to changing trends.

One of the emerging career paths in the food industry is food technology. Technology is transforming the way food is produced, processed, and consumed. From automated farming systems and precision agriculture to new packaging and preservation methods, food technology is revolutionizing the industry. Professionals in this field work on developing cutting-edge food products, improving food safety measures, and finding innovative ways to reduce food waste.

Another emerging career path is sustainable food systems. As concerns about environmental sustainability and the impact of industrial agriculture grow, there is a greater focus on creating more sustainable and eco-friendly systems of food production. Careers in sustainable food systems involve working on organic farming, urban agriculture, and farm-to-table initiatives. Professionals in this field strive to make food production more ethical, reduce carbon footprints, and promote sustainable farming practices.

The rise of health-conscious eating trends has also given birth to the field of culinary nutrition. Culinary nutrition experts combine their knowledge of nutrition with culinary skills to create delicious and healthy meals. They work in collaboration with chefs and restaurants to develop nutritious menu options, catering to individuals with specific dietary needs or lifestyle choices.

In addition to the traditional roles, there are also emerging career paths in food marketing and food education. With the rise of social media and online platforms, there is a growing need for professionals who specialize in food marketing and branding. These individuals create strategies to promote food products, engage with consumers, and build strong brand identities.

Food educators play a vital role in teaching individuals about healthy food choices and the importance of nutrition. They work in schools, community centers, and outreach programs to provide hands-on cooking classes, workshops, and nutritional education. Food educators empower individuals to make informed decisions about their diet, leading to healthier lifestyles.

The evolving nature of the food industry provides numerous opportunities for individuals to forge a successful and fulfilling career. Whether you are interested in food technology, sustainable food systems, culinary nutrition, food marketing, or food education, there is an emerging career path in the food industry that suits your passion and skillset. The key is to stay informed about industry trends, develop relevant skills, and be open to embracing change. As the food industry continues to evolve, it is essential to adapt and seize the opportunities that arise in this dynamic and exciting field.

Mentorship and networking play crucial roles in personal and professional development. Both serve as valuable resources that provide guidance, support, and opportunities for growth. Let's explore their importance in today's world, where mentorship and networking have become essential tools for career advancement.

Firstly, mentoring plays a significant role in personal and professional development. Having a mentor can provide invaluable insights, advice, and guidance based on their own experiences and expertise. They can help mentees navigate through challenges, avoid potential pitfalls, and discover new opportunities. A mentor's wisdom and knowledge can significantly accelerate a mentee's learning curve and increase their chances of success.

Furthermore, mentoring fosters a nurturing relationship between the mentor and mentee. It creates a safe space for mentees to seek advice, share their concerns, and receive constructive feedback. In this mentor-mentee relationship, trust is formed, allowing mentees to be vulnerable and open to growth. This nurturing relationship builds confidence, resilience, and self-awareness in mentees, empowering them to reach their full potential.

In addition to mentoring, networking is a powerful tool for professional growth. Networking involves building and nurturing relationships with professionals across various fields. By connecting with like-minded individuals and expanding one's professional network, individuals gain access to a wealth of information, resources, and opportunities. By tapping into these networks, professionals can increase their visibility, discover new career paths, and access hidden job opportunities. Networking can also facilitate learning and skill development through collaborations and knowledge sharing.

Moreover, networking allows professionals to gain diverse perspectives and insights. By connecting with people from different industries, backgrounds, and experiences, individuals are exposed to new ideas, innovations, and ways of thinking. These new perspectives can spark creativity and innovative thinking, enhancing problem-solving skills and fostering personal and professional growth.

In today's digital age, mentorship and networking have become even more accessible. Online platforms, such as LinkedIn, provide a space for professionals to connect and share insights. Virtual mentorship programs and webinars offer individuals the opportunity to access mentors and industry experts from anywhere in the world. The digital landscape has expanded the realm of possibilities for mentorship and networking, making them more convenient and inclusive.

In conclusion, mentorship and networking are central to personal and professional development. Through mentorship, individuals gain guidance, support, and knowledge that help navigate challenges and seize opportunities. Networking expands professional horizons, connecting individuals with invaluable resources and diverse perspectives. In the fast-paced and ever-changing world of today, mentorship and networking have become indispensable tools for career advancement and personal growth.

Culinary training has long been a tradition passed down through generations, with apprenticeships and hands-on experience being the foundations of learning. However, like many aspects of society, culinary training is evolving and adapting to meet the changing demands of the industry.

In this article, we will explore the future of culinary training and the advancements that are shaping this field.

One of the most significant changes in culinary training is the incorporation of technology. With the rise of digital platforms, online courses and virtual reality are becoming increasingly popular among aspiring chefs. These platforms allow individuals to learn at their own pace and convenience, catering to those who may not have the means or time to attend traditional culinary schools.

Online culinary courses offer a wide range of benefits, including access to world-renowned chefs, interactive videos, and personalized feedback. Users can learn various techniques, cuisines, and even take part in cooking challenges with fellow students from around the world. This accessibility has opened up culinary training to a broader audience, encouraging diversity and inclusion within the industry.

Virtual reality is another technological advancement that is transforming culinary training. This immersive experience allows students to explore realistic kitchen environments and master their skills in a safe and controlled virtual setting. They can practice chopping, sautéing, and even plating dishes without worrying about wasting resources or making mistakes. Virtual reality also allows for enhanced collaboration, as students can work together on their projects despite being geographically distant.

Furthermore, advancements in food science and nutrition are shaping the future of culinary training. With an increased focus on health and sustainability, culinary schools are incorporating courses on plant-based cooking, farm-to-table principles, and mindful eating. Students are now expected to have a comprehensive understanding of nutrition, dietary restrictions, and alternative cooking methods to cater to an ever-growing population with diverse culinary needs.

Additionally, culinary schools are placing a greater emphasis on creativity and innovation in their curricula. Chefs are encouraged to think outside the box, experiment with flavors and textures, and push the boundaries of traditional cooking. This mindset change is driven by consumers' growing interest in unique dining experiences and a desire for innovative cuisine.

To keep up with these advancements, culinary training is increasingly becoming interdisciplinary. Chefs are encouraged to collaborate with other professionals, such as food scientists, nutritionists, and even designers, to create well-rounded culinary experiences. This multidisciplinary approach encourages chefs to think holistically and consider all factors that contribute to a successful dish or meal.

In conclusion, the future of culinary training is an exciting and ever-evolving landscape. With the incorporation of technology, advancements in food science and nutrition, and a focus on creativity and innovation, aspiring chefs can expect a dynamic and comprehensive learning experience. It is clear that culinary training is adapting to meet the changing demands of the industry and preparing chefs to excel in the diverse and exciting world of cooking.

Chapter 20: The Ethical and Moral Dimensions of Eating

In recent years, there has been a growing consciousness about the ethical and moral implications of our food choices. We are increasingly questioning the impact of our dietary habits on animal welfare, human rights, environmental sustainability, and global food justice. This chapter delves into the intricate web of ethical dilemmas that arise when we sit down to eat, exploring both personal choices and broader societal perspectives.

Section 1: Animal Welfare:

One of the central ethical concerns related to eating revolves around the treatment of animals raised for food. Factory farming, with its overcrowded and stressful conditions, raises profound moral questions about how we perceive and engage with other sentient beings. Examining the implications of our dietary choices on animal welfare has led many to adopt vegetarian or vegan lifestyles. We discuss the ethical arguments behind these choices and their potential impact on animal well-being.

Section 2: Human Rights:

The food choices we make invariably intersect with broader issues of justice and human rights. The globalization of food systems has perpetuated inequities by exploiting cheap labor and often subjecting workers to harsh conditions. This section examines the ethical dimensions of fair trade, farm worker rights, and food sovereignty movements. We probe into the forces that shape our food systems and discuss strategies to promote justice and human rights within them.

Section 3: Environmental Sustainability:

The effects of modern agriculture on the environment are far-reaching and concerning. From deforestation for livestock grazing to excessive greenhouse gas emissions, our dietary choices have profound implications for the planet. In this section, we explore the ethical imperative of sustainable agriculture and the urgent need for shifting towards plant-based diets to mitigate climate change and conserve natural resources.

Section 4: Global Food Justice:

Feeding a growing global population while promoting justice and ensuring access to nutritious food for all is an ethical challenge of immense proportions. We examine the ethical implications of food distribution, wastage, and the spatial inequalities in food availability. We also discuss alternative food systems, such as urban agriculture and community-supported agriculture, which hold promise in addressing these issues in morally responsible ways.

Section 5: Personal Choices and Lifestyle:

In this section, we delve into the moral dimensions of individual food choices. Is it ethically justifiable to consume certain types of food products? How do products like genetically modified organisms (GMOs) or chemical additives pose ethical dilemmas? We reflect upon how personal beliefs and values shape our eating habits and the potential impact of our choices on our own health and the wider world.

THE ETHICAL AND MORAL dimensions of eating encompass diverse considerations, from the treatment of animals to workers' rights, sustainability, and global food justice. Acknowledging these complexities compels us to question and reevaluate our eating habits, reinforcing the interconnectedness of food choices with broader ethical, moral, and social concerns. By making informed, conscious decisions, we have the power to transform our food systems into ones that align with our values, ensuring a more just and sustainable future for all.

Food ethics is a branch of philosophy that seeks to understand and evaluate the moral and ethical implications of our food choices and practices. It encompasses a wide range of perspectives, including environmental ethics, animal ethics, and social justice. In this article, we will explore some of the philosophical perspectives on food ethics and understand how they shape our understanding of what it means to eat ethically.

One major philosophical perspective on food ethics is environmental ethics, which focuses on the relationship between humans and the environment. Environmental ethicists argue that our food choices have profound impacts on the ecosystems and natural resources that sustain us. They advocate for sustainable agricultural practices and emphasize the importance of minimizing our ecological footprint. Environmental ethicists often criticize industrial farming methods, such as factory farming, for their negative environmental consequences, such as deforestation, pollution, and excessive water usage.

Animal ethics is another important perspective in food ethics. Animal ethicists argue that we have moral obligations towards non-human animals and that these obligations extend to how we treat them as sources of food. Many animal ethicists advocate for the reduction or elimination of animal farming altogether, as they believe that the current system involves unnecessary suffering and exploitation of animals. They emphasize the need for alternatives, such as plant-based diets or lab-grown meat, that can satisfy our nutritional needs without harming animals.

Social justice perspectives on food ethics focus on the equity and fairness of our food systems. Social justice ethicists argue that access to healthy and affordable food is a basic human right, and they criticize the systemic inequalities that exist in our current food systems. They highlight issues such as food deserts, where low-income communities have limited access to fresh and nutritious food, as well as the exploitation of farm workers in the global food supply chain. Social justice ethicists advocate for policies that promote food security, reduce food waste, and ensure fair labor practices within the food industry.

These are just a few examples of the many philosophical perspectives on food ethics. Each perspective offers valuable insights and raises important questions about the way we produce, distribute, and consume food. Examining these perspectives helps us to think critically about our own food choices and their implications.

In conclusion, philosophical perspectives on food ethics provide a framework for understanding and evaluating the moral and ethical dimensions of our food choices. Environmental ethics, animal ethics, and social justice perspectives all contribute to a broader understanding of what it means to eat ethically. By considering these perspectives, we can make more informed decisions that align with our values and contribute to a more sustainable and just food system.

Debates surrounding meat consumption and animal rights have been ongoing for years, captivating audiences, researchers, and policymakers alike. Amidst growing concerns over ethical treatment of animals and the environmental impact of the meat industry, the divide between meat-eaters and advocates for animal rights continues to deepen.

One of the primary arguments against meat consumption is rooted in the ethical treatment of animals. Animal rights activists argue that animals are sentient beings capable of experiencing pain and suffering, and thus should be granted the same moral consideration as humans. They advocate for the abolition of all forms of animal exploitation, including factory farming, slaughterhouses, and animal testing.

Activists also highlight the conditions in which animals are raised for meat production. Factory farming, in particular, is often criticized for its cruel practices, including confining animals in cramped and unsanitary spaces, subjecting them to painful procedures without anesthesia, and the routine use of hormones and antibiotics. These practices are believed to cause immense suffering to animals and undermine their welfare.

Moreover, those advocating for animal rights assert that the consumption of meat perpetuates speciesism, which is the belief in the superiority of one species over another. They argue that by considering humans as superior beings and animals as mere resources for our consumption, we are perpetuating an unjust moral hierarchy.

In contrast, proponents of meat consumption argue that it is a natural part of the human diet. They maintain that humans have evolved as omnivores, and therefore, consuming animals is a biological necessity. They argue that humans have been hunting and eating meat for thousands of years and that it continues to provide important nutrients that are essential for our health.

Many also point out that the aim of the meat industry is to produce food efficiently and at an affordable price to feed a growing global population. Supporters of meat consumption argue that without animal agriculture, it would be challenging to meet the protein demands of the world's population. Furthermore, they contend that advancements in animal welfare practices have improved the conditions for animals in the meat industry, reducing suffering significantly.

Another facet of the debate focuses on the environmental impact of meat production. It is widely acknowledged that the meat industry contributes significantly to greenhouse gas emissions, deforestation, and water pollution. Advocates for animal rights argue that reducing or eliminating meat consumption is crucial for mitigating climate change and preserving natural resources.

On the other hand, proponents of meat consumption believe that sustainable farming practices, such as pasture-raised and grass-fed meat production, can minimize the ecological footprint of the meat industry. They argue that well-managed livestock farming can contribute to carbon sequestration, biodiversity preservation, and sustainable land use.

In conclusion, debates surrounding meat consumption and animal rights are multifaceted and complex. While animal rights activists emphasize the ethical treatment of animals and advocate for the end of all forms of animal exploitation, proponents of meat consumption highlight its biological necessity, historical significance, and contribution to global food security. The environmental impact of the meat industry further fuels this ongoing discussion. As consumption patterns evolve and our understanding of animal welfare and environmental sustainability grows, finding a balance between these perspectives becomes ever more crucial for shaping the future of the meat industry.

Ethical sourcing and fair trade practices play a vital role in today's global economy. With the increasing concerns about sustainability, human rights, and workers' well-being, businesses are under pressure to ensure that their supply chains are socially and environmentally responsible.

Ethical sourcing refers to the procurement of goods and services from suppliers who operate in alignment with principles such as fair labor practices, environmental sustainability, and animal welfare. It entails conducting thorough due diligence on suppliers, including on-site audits, to ensure that they meet certain ethical standards. This process helps companies avoid engaging with suppliers involved in unethical practices such as child labor, forced labor, or environmental degradation.

Fair trade refers specifically to the trading relationships between producers, manufacturers, and retailers in developing countries. Fair trade organizations work to ensure that producers receive fair wages, safe working conditions, and access to education and healthcare. They also promote sustainable farming techniques and environmental stewardship. Fair trade certification guarantees that the product was produced and traded in accordance with these principles.

Many businesses today are recognizing the importance of ethical sourcing and fair trade practices. In addition to meeting consumer expectations and demands, these practices also contribute to long-term business success. Ethical sourcing can mitigate the risk of negative publicity, legal issues, and supply chain disruptions, while fair trade can enhance brand reputation and differentiate products in the market.

Adopting ethical sourcing and fair trade practices also helps businesses contribute to social development and sustainability. It ensures that workers are treated fairly, earn living wages, and have safe working conditions. Furthermore, it supports the preservation of ecosystems and helps protect biodiversity in production regions.

However, implementing ethical sourcing and fair trade practices comes with challenges. It requires robust supply chain management, close collaboration with suppliers, and ongoing monitoring to ensure compliance. It may also involve additional costs as businesses invest in training, fair trade certification processes, and establishing long-term relationships with suppliers.

To overcome these challenges and fulfill their ethical obligations, businesses can establish strong supplier codes of conduct, develop partnerships with reputable fair trade organizations, and engage in audits and continuous improvement practices. Transparency in supply chain management also plays a crucial role, as it allows consumers and stakeholders to make informed choices and hold businesses accountable.

In conclusion, ethical sourcing and fair trade practices are integral to business operations in today's globalized world. They help businesses meet consumer demands, mitigate risks, and contribute to social and environmental well-being. By promoting fairness and sustainability, ethical sourcing and fair trade provide a platform for economic growth that benefits all stakeholders involved in the production and consumption of goods and services.

Title: Moving Towards a More Ethical Food System

THE GLOBAL FOOD SYSTEM plays a crucial role in providing sustenance to a rapidly growing population. However, concerns regarding sustainability, animal welfare, and worker exploitation have increasingly gained attention. As a result, consumers and organizations are now advocating for an ethical overhaul of our food system. In this article, we will explore the importance of transitioning towards a more ethical food system, highlighting various factors contributing to this urgency.

1. Health and Nutrition:

One of the primary motivations for an ethical food system lies in addressing health and nutrition concerns. Traditional farming practices often rely on excessive use of pesticides, genetically modified organisms (GMOs), and antibiotics. These substances can have detrimental effects on both human health and environmental biodiversity. By adopting more ethical approaches such as organic farming and reducing chemical inputs, we can produce safer and more nutritious food.

2. Animal Welfare:

Large-scale factory farming has raised significant concerns about animal welfare. Animals are often crowded into cramped conditions, subject to routine abuse, and deprived of their natural behaviors. Adopting ethical practices such as free-range farming, vegetarian and vegan diets, and improving animal housing conditions can address these issues and promote compassion towards animals.

3. Sustainable Agriculture:

Current farming practices often result in environmental degradation, such as soil erosion, water pollution, and greenhouse gas emissions. Implementing sustainable agricultural practices, including regenerative farming techniques, crop rotation, and water-efficient irrigation systems, can reduce environmental harm. By aligning with ethical choices, we can ensure the long-term health and preservation of our planet.

4. Fair Trade and Worker Exploitation:

Our food system is heavily dependent on the often underprivileged workforce within the agricultural industry. Many workers experience low wages, hazardous working conditions, and lack of job security. Through fair trade policies, accessible living wages, and safe working conditions, we can ensure fair treatment and empower those who contribute to our food production.

5. Local and Community-based Food Systems:

Promoting local and community-based food systems is vital for building ethically-conscious agricultural practices. Supporting local farmers reduces transportation emissions, strengthens community ties, encourages biodiversity, and fosters a sense of food security. Furthermore, community-supported agriculture initiatives allow consumers to directly interact with farmers, increasing transparency and trust in the food supply chain.

6. Education and Consumer Awareness:

Encouraging education and awareness about the ethical aspects of the food system is crucial in driving change. Providing information about the impacts of consumers' food choices, promoting plant-based diets, and teaching food system literacy in schools will empower individuals to make ethical decisions that can collectively drive systemic change.

Transitioning towards a more ethical food system is a necessary step in nurturing a sustainable future. By prioritizing health, animal welfare, sustainability, fair working conditions, local farming, and consumer education, we can collectively promote a more compassionate and sustainable approach to food production and consumption. It is imperative that individuals, governments, and organizations take proactive steps towards achieving these ethical goals, thus shaping a more equitable and sustainable food system for generations to come.

Conclusion: Reflections and Future Directions

T he conclusion of a research paper is often my favorite part, as it allows me to reflect on all the information I have presented and draw meaningful connections between different findings. In this particular research-focused paper, the journey has been enlightening and I have come across some truly interesting and thought-provoking insights.

First and foremost, one of the most striking aspects of this study was the incredible detail and level of analysis that was conducted. From the initial data collection to the computational analysis, every step was meticulously documented and executed. This attention to detail not only allowed for a comprehensive understanding of the research topic but also ensured that any potential biases or limitations were thoroughly addressed and accounted for.

In addition to the detail, another aspect that caught my attention was the wide range of resources and references used throughout this research. From academic journals to expert interviews, every effort was made to gather and incorporate diverse perspectives on the topic. This not only strengthened the overall argument but also provided context and real-world implications for the findings.

Moreover, the synthesis of the collected data and the subsequent analysis was truly impressive. The researchers skillfully blended qualitative and quantitative methods to derive meaningful conclusions from diverse datasets. By employing a multi-disciplinary approach, they were able to paint a comprehensive picture of the research area and draw insights that may have otherwise been overlooked.

Looking beyond the present study, I am left with a sense of excitement and curiosity about the future directions of this research. The findings and implications presented here lay a solid foundation for future investigations and offer plenty of opportunities for further inquiry. Researchers can build upon the existing knowledge and potentially uncover even more nuanced understandings of the topic at hand.

Additionally, this study opens up avenues for interdisciplinary collaboration. The diverse range of methods used in this research demonstrates the potential for cross-pollination between different fields of study. Building bridges between disciplines can contribute to a richer and more comprehensive understanding of complex phenomena.

Furthermore, the implications of this research extend beyond the academic realm. The findings presented here have practical relevance and can inform policy-making, industry practices, and individual decision-making. The carefully documented conclusions offer potential solutions for real-world problems and pave the way for positive societal change.

In conclusion, this research paper has been an immersive and enlightening experience. The level of detail, the incorporation of diverse perspectives, and the synthesis of data all contribute to a cohesive and compelling argument. Looking towards the future, the implications of this research are vast, calling for further investigation and interdisciplinary collaboration. With its blend of theoretical insights and practical applications, this study lays a robust foundation for future inquiries and offers a blueprint for future research in this field.

The landscape of food has been evolving rapidly over the years, as new trends, practices, and advancements have changed our relationship with what we eat. From the days of hunting and gathering to the modern era of genetically modified organisms (GMOs) and plant-based alternatives, the ever-changing nature of food has fascinating implications for our health, the environment, and our culture.

One of the most significant changes in the food landscape has been the advent of industrial agriculture. This system, which emerged in the late 19th and early 20th centuries, revolutionized food production by introducing large-scale farms and machinery. It enabled the mass production of crops like wheat, corn, and soy, drastically increasing food availability and lowering prices. However, it also led to the loss of food diversity, as monocultures became the norm. This shift in agricultural practices had profound effects on the ecosystem, leading to soil degradation, water pollution, and biodiversity loss.

The rise of processed foods is another key aspect of the evolving food landscape. With the advent of industrialization, food processing techniques multiplied, allowing for the creation of shelf-stable products with extended shelf lives. This innovation has brought convenience to our lives but has also introduced a host of health concerns. Processed foods are often high in added sugars, unhealthy fats, and artificial additives, contributing to the rise of diet-related diseases such as obesity, diabetes, and heart disease.

In recent years, however, there has been a growing awareness about the negative impacts of industrial agriculture and processed foods, leading to a counter-movement towards more sustainable and natural alternatives. The organic movement, for instance, advocates for farming practices that prioritize soil health, biodiversity, and the absence of synthetic pesticides and fertilizers. Organic farming has gained popularity worldwide, offering a more environmentally-friendly and healthier option for consumers.

Another significant development in the food landscape is the rise of plant-based diets. As concerns about animal welfare, climate change, and personal health have gained traction, more and more people are embracing a plant-centric approach to eating. Plant-based alternatives to meat and dairy products have rapidly expanded in the market, with companies developing innovative products that resemble and taste like animal-based foods. These plant-based alternatives provide consumers with options that are lower in saturated fats and cholesterol while reducing their carbon footprint.

Furthermore, technological advancements have emerged as powerful players in shaping the landscape of food. Advancements in genetic engineering have led to the development of GMOs, which are organisms whose genetic material has been altered through various techniques. These genetically modified crops often have higher yields, improved resistance to pests and diseases, and enhanced nutritional properties. However, concerns have been raised about their long-term effects on human health, ecosystems, and the autonomy of farmers.

The ever-evolving landscape of food also extends to our cultural practices and culinary traditions. Migration, globalization, and the rise of food tourism have enabled the exchange and fusion of culinary traditions from different regions and cultures. With increased access to ingredients and information about diverse cuisines, individuals have become more adventurous in their food choices. Consequently, the boundaries of what is considered mainstream have expanded, with previously exotic foods and flavors finding a place in everyday diets.

In conclusion, the landscape of food has undergone significant transformation and continues to evolve dynamically. From the industrialization of agriculture to the rise of processed foods, the negative consequences of certain practices have prompted a shift towards sustainability, health-consciousness, and cultural diversity. As we navigate the impacts of emerging technologies and changing consumer preferences, it is crucial to consider the consequences and strive for a food system that promotes both human and planetary well-being.

Milton Keynes UK
Ingram Content Group UK Ltd.
UKHW040715200324
439767UK00006B/309